An Illustrated History of

CARDIFF DOCKS

Volume 3

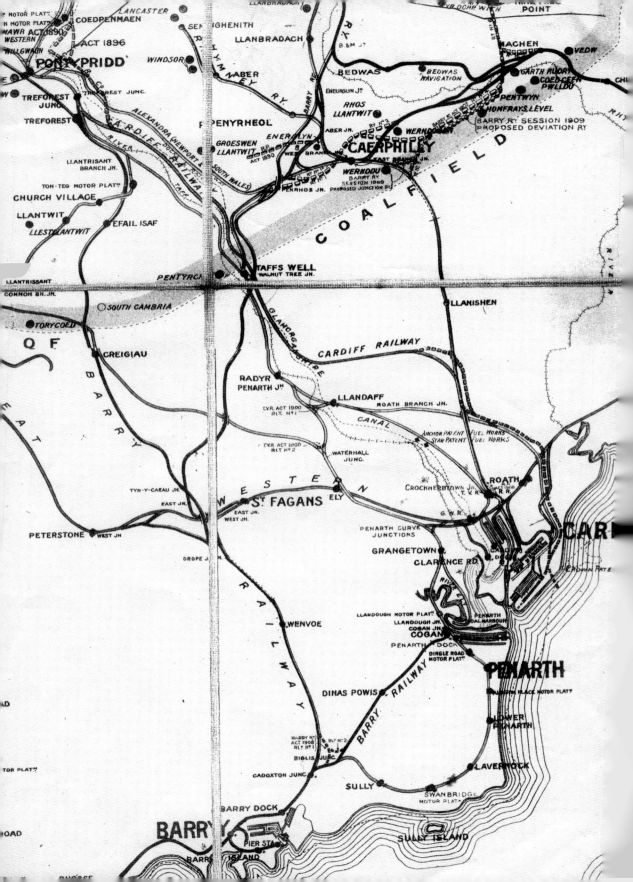

An Illustrated History of

CARDIFF DOCKS

Volume 3:
The Cardiff Railway Company
and the docks at war

John Hutton

·MARITIME HERITAGE·
from
The NOSTALGIA Collection

This work is dedicated to my sister, Joyce Sandra Hutton,
to the new addition to the family, my grandson Aled, and to my cousins
in the USA, Joe and Gladys Moore, and their son Dale.

© John Hutton 2009

First published in 2009

British Library Cataloguing in
Publication Data

A catalogue record for this book is
available from the British Library.

ISBN 978 1 85794 309 2

Silver Link Publishing Ltd
The Trundle
Ringstead Road
Great Addington
Kettering
Northants NN14 4BW

Tel/Fax: 01536 330588
email: sales@nostalgiacollection.com
Website: www.nostalgiacollection.com

Printed and bound in the Czech Republic

A Silver Link book
from
The NOSTALGIA *Collection*

Half title   The crest of the Cardiff Railway Company.
Author's collection

Page 2   A Cardiff Railway Company map of 1904. The
broken line beside and above Cardiff is the route of the
proposed new line that would have linked up with the main
line west of Heath Junction, but this idea eventually fell by
the wayside and was withdrawn. *Author's collection*

Below   This cast iron Cardiff Railway sign was photographed
at Heath (Low Level) Halt on Saturday 31 October 1953.
J. and J. Collection

CONTENTS

Cardiff Railway 0-6-0T No 7 travels bunker-first with a railmotor attached at Heath Halt on 17 May 1919. *LCGB (Ken Nunn Collection)*

Cardiff Docks at war: on the north side of Bute East Dock No 2 branch, on the night of 3/4 March 1941, high-explosive bombs caused damage to the permanent way, telephone communications and the Wagon Repairs premises. In the background is the silhouette of the GKN steelworks. *Associated British Ports*

INTRODUCTION

The origin of the Cardiff Railway Company is entwined with the history and growth of Cardiff as a major coal port. Over many years the Bute Docks Company, and before it the Bute Trustees, had skilfully managed the railway traffic entering and leaving the docks, which included maintenance of the running lines and sidings, signal boxes, capstans, coaling hoists and cranes, warehouses, storage conditions, cattle lairs and the many other aspects connected with the docks. The third and fourth Marquises of Bute had been content to allow other railway companies to enter the docks, together with the massive tonnage of coal traffic that they carried from the numerous collieries in the valleys of South Wales. And it was from these docks that vessels sailed heavily laden, taking the black mineral to all corners of the globe. Thus Cardiff Docks, accommodating more than 120 miles of track, all of which was condensed into an area covering a little more than a single square mile of land, supplied the world market.

But change was coming. The Taff Vale Railway Company had built additional and alternative dock accommodation at Penarth, on the River Ely, as early as 1859, followed by the opening of Penarth Docks in 1865, enlarged in 1884. A further threat to Cardiff's position, and one of major importance, came in the form of the Barry Docks & Railway Company, whose Act was passed in 1884.

Under this pressure, and with the very real risk of losing their mineral traffic, the Directors of the Bute Docks Company decided to build a railway of their own, connecting with the Taff Vale Railway at Treforest. At the same time a change of name to the Cardiff Railway Company was sanctioned, legalised by an Act of Parliament on 6 August 1897.

The route chosen was a difficult one, but there was no alternative. In 1898 a series of negotiations took place between the Cardiff Railway Company and the Glamorganshire Canal owners to take over of their canal, draining the water from it, and laying the railway along its route; by this date there had been continuous and drastic losses in water traffic on the canal. However, the railway was not allowed to do this, so the first section of line was laid from a junction with the Rhymney Railway at Heath to Tongwynlais, a distance of 4 miles. The line then headed northwards from Tongwynlais, running parallel with the TVR lines, using the valley of the Taff. The greatest geological problems arose where the route squeezed its way through the Nantgarw Gap at Taffs Well, for already using it were the River Taff, the Cardiff Road, the remains of the Glamorganshire Canal and the lines of the Taff Vale Railway; the

The seal of the Cardiff Railway Company, 1886-1897 (photographed at the GWR Museum, Swindon), was just one of many seals that came into the possession of the GWR with the passing of the 1921 Railways Act. *Author*

Right A Railway Clearing House map of 1920, showing the route of the Cardiff Railway from Heath Junction to Taffs Well. Also shown on the map is the route of the Glamorganshire Canal, along which the Cardiff Railway hoped to lay their initial line, a hope that was eventually dashed by Parliament. *A. G. Powell collection*

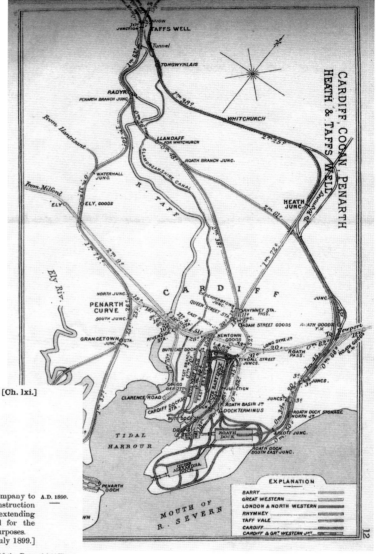

[82 & 63 VICT.]   *Cardiff Railway Act, 1899.*   [Ch. lxi.]

CHAPTER lxi.

An Act for empowering the Cardiff Railway Company to A.D. 1899. construct new Railways and to abandon the construction of portions of railways already authorised for extending the time for the purchase of lands for and for the completion of certain railways and for other purposes.

[13th July 1899.]

WHEREAS under the Bute Docks (Transfer) Act 1886 the Bute 49 & 50 Vict. Docks Company were incorporated and became the owners c. lxxxvi. of the Bute Docks at Cardiff in the county of Glamorgan :

And whereas by the Cardiff Railway Act 1897 (herein-after 60 & 61 Vict. called " the Act of 1897 ") the Company were authorised to construct c. ccvii. certain railways in the county of Glamorgan and the name of the company was changed and is now the Cardiff Railway Company in this Act called " the Company " :

And whereas by the Cardiff Railway Act 1898 (herein-after called 61 & 62 Vict. " the Act of 1898 ") the Company were empowered to construct c. celxii. the lines of railway therein described :

And whereas the position of portions of those lines as authorised may advantageously be varied and it is expedient to sanction the abandonment of the construction of those portions as well as of part of a railway authorised by the Bute Docks Act 1894 (herein-after called " the Act of 1894 ") and of part of a railway authorised by the Act of 1897 :

And whereas it would be of public and local advantage to empower the Company to construct the lines of railway in this Act described :

And whereas by the Great Western Railway Act 1896 (in this Act called " the Great Western Act of 1896 ") the Great Western Railway Company (in this Act called " the Great Western Company ") were authorised to construct (among others) a railway therein described as Railway No. 1 and in this Act referred to as " the Great Western Railway No. 1 " :

[*Price* 1s. 6d.]   A   1

Left The Act of Parliament empowering the Cardiff Railway Company to construct new railways and to abandon the construction of previously proposed railway undertakings, dated 13 July 1899. *Associated British Ports*

Right Cardiff District map of 1910, showing the proposed but subsequently unbuilt Cardiff Railway routes: Nos 2 (1903 Act), 3 (1898 Act), 5 (1899 Act), 6 (1899 Act) and 7 (1899 Act). *Author's collection*

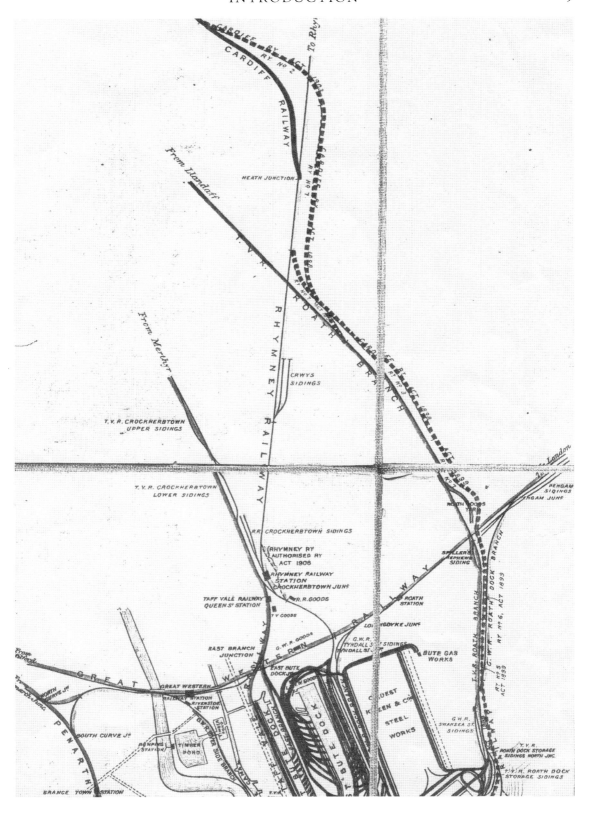

Rhymney Railway also ran down the mountain side to make its junction at Taffs Well, while the Barry Railway crossed the valley on a viaduct supported by huge stone pillars. All in all, therefore, it was a very tight gap indeed, but for the Cardiff Railway to reach its destination – the connection with the TVR at Treforest – this part of the route was an obstacle that had to be surpassed.

An interview appeared in *The Railway Magazine*, Volume 23 of 1908, describing the building of the line:

'Of British ports that owe their existence and prosperity to railway enterprise, there are many, but in the case of the Bute Docks and the Cardiff Railway the positions are reversed, and instead of the docks being constructed to feed the railway, the railway was made, and in some part is still being made, to provide facilities for the traffic to and from the docks, a policy which received considerable impetus when the opening of the Barry Dock & Railway diverted large quantities of traffic from the Bute Docks.

In 1897, after a strenuous fight with opposing interests, parliamentary powers were obtained by the Bute Docks Company for the construction of five branch railways, some 12 miles in extent, and thus the Cardiff Railway was inaugurated. The authorised mileage of the Cardiff Railway at the present time is about 18 miles, while the dock railways, located within an area of 1 square mile, comprise a system of some 120 miles.

The main line of the Cardiff Railway is still under construction. Commencing some 2½ miles from Cardiff Docks at Heath Junction, it joins the Taff Vale Railway's main line south of Treforest Junction, a run of 11 miles. There is also a junction from the main line to Pontypridd Station (TVR) for passengers and goods traffic. It is intended to join the main line north of Heath Junction, to give direct access to the Bute Docks. The construction of the line has been a lengthy business owing to the many engineering difficulties to be overcome. Its completion will do much to develop the district it will serve, as well as to carry out the premier purpose of its construction, that is the conveyance of coal from the Taff Vale Railway and other points to Cardiff Docks.

The status of Cardiff as the premier port in the world for the shipment of coal, and the first port in the United Kingdom for shipping cleared to foreign countries and British possessions, received royal recognition by the visit of King Edward on 13 July 1907, to open the Queen Alexandra Dock, the provision of which was rendering requisite and necessary by the ever growing traffic of the port. The railways, other than the Cardiff Railway, having communication with the docks are the London & North Western, Great Western, Midland, Taff Vale, Rhymney, Brecon & Merthyr, and the Pontypridd, Caerphilly & Newport line. The latter line was in 1897 taken over by the Alexandra (Newport & South Wales) Docks & Railway Company.'

An extract from Bradshaw's timetable of July 1922. *Author's collection*

THE CARDIFF RAILWAY: HEATH JUNCTION TO TREFOREST

In 1898 the contractors, Messrs Monk & Newell of Liverpool, started work on their stretch of line (contract No 1) from Heath Junction to Tongwynlais, shifting nearly 2 million cubic yards of rock and soil and using hundreds of thousands of bricks to construct the line, which also included five occupational level crossings. They completed their contract on 30 January 1902. The remainder of the line, including the junction at Treforest (contract No 2) went to Messrs Thomas Oliver & Sons of Westminster in December 1904, and this work was completed in 1907. The line was a superb achievement, constructed with double track throughout and including a total of 27 bridges, of which 15 were overbridges, built on a skew in most cases, and a viaduct, with a tunnel at Tongwynlais 325 feet long, located directly beneath Castell Coch ('Red Castle'), also owned by the Marquis of Bute. Because of the steep slopes encountered, some 10 retaining walls and 15 cuttings were needed, and in addition the River Taff had to be diverted near Nantgarw – all this for a line that would run for a distance of less than 9 miles. The first stations were provided at Whitchurch, Tongwynlais, Glan-y-Llyn and Upper Boat, and halts were provided at Heath, Coryton, Rhiwbina, Nantgarw and Rhydyfelin. A further halt at Birchgrove was opened in 1929 by the GWR, when housing development along the main road made it a suitable site.

Contract No 2 ended at the boundary of a piece of land owned by the Taff Vale Railway at Treforest, and thus started a bitter feud, with the will of one great company pitched against the will of another.

In the *Railway & Travel Monthly Magazine* of April 1911, an interview was given to Mr G. A. Sekon, from which the following extracts are taken:

'The opening of the Cardiff Railway for passenger traffic on 1 March from Heath Junction, north of the Cardiff Station of the Rhymney Railway, to Rhyd-y-felin, near Treforest, marked an important departure in the history of this undertaking. The "20th-century development" of the Cardiff Railway is almost the complete history of the Cardiff Railway, which was only incorporated on 6 August 1897, although portions of the Cardiff Docks, which form an important part of the property of the Cardiff Railway, had been in use for many years, the Bute Dock as long ago as 1837. In connection with this dock there was about 130 miles of railways, which, as the dock estate has grown, and the docks have increased, has also extended and junctions were made with the Great Western Railway, Taff Vale Railway, and the Rhymney Railway. Locomotives were provided by the Marquis of Bute (the owner of these docks, prior to the incorporation of the Cardiff Railway) for the purpose of dealing with the coal and other traffic brought to the docks by the railway companies mentioned. The Queen Alexandra Dock, which is the largest dock at Cardiff, is a "20th-century development" of the Cardiff Railway, which we shall refer to after dealing with the railway itself. The connection between the new railway and the dock lines of the Cardiff Railway is by means of running powers over the Rhymney Railway. At present it is not proposed to run the Cardiff Railway's passenger service to and from the docks; the trains will terminate at, and start from, the Rhymney Railway's Cardiff Station.

Leaving the Rhymney Railway at Heath Junction, 1 mile 72 chains from the Rhymney

Railway's Station, the new railway terminates by a junction with the Taff Vale Railway at Treforest. Many physical difficulties were met with in the construction of the line, but the skill of the engineers successfully surmounted them. The new railway passes along the Taff Valley (already occupied by the River Taff, the Merthyr main road, the Glamorganshire Canal and the Taff Vale Railway), so that much ingenuity was required to find room for the Cardiff Railway.

There are four passenger stations and five halts on the new line. From Cardiff these are as follows: The Heath (halt), Rhubina (halt), Whitchurch, Coryton (halt), Tongwynlais, Glan-y-Llyn, Nantgarw (halt), Upper Boat (halt), and Rhyd-y-felin (halt)… The docks belonging to the Cardiff Railway consist of five docks proper, the Bute West Dock, with a water area of 19½ acres, Bute East Dock (46¼ acres), Roath Dock (33 acres), Roath Basin (12 acres), and the Queen Alexandra Dock, which is the largest of the five, having 52 acres.

The docks, since their opening in 1840, have gone ahead amazingly, the imports for 1910 amounting to 1,854,430 tons, the exports being 10,327,765 tons. The Bute Docks (as the docks of the Cardiff Railway are usually called) are not dependent alone on the exportation of coal for revenue; they are the docks in South Wales licensed by the Board of Trade for the importation of one of the staple food products of the British Isles, ie cattle. The Roath Dock has been selected to deal with this traffic, and cattle lairs have been provided alongside the lock leading to this dock. Adjacent to these lairs are the abattoirs, from whence the carcases of the slaughtered cattle pass to the chill rooms, or maybe to the delivery passage. Cold storage plant of the cold blast type is also fitted to the jetty warehouse. Although naturally enough a large portion of the frozen meat handled at Bute Docks goes to feed the crowded population of South Wales, much of it is despatched in refrigerator vans to distant parts of the kingdom, Birmingham and district coming in for a large share of the traffic. Fruit and various other food stuffs also

find their way to this great industrial centre through these docks, while Cardiff has now the largest import trade in potatoes in the United Kingdom. Grain of various sorts is also extensively handled, one warehouse being sufficient to hold 50,000 quarters at one time. Into this dock, too, come the timber vessels from all parts, conveying principally pit wood and mining timber, for use in the mines of the South Wales coalfield. Teak and other timbers, including railway sleepers and ships' timber, also arrive at this dock in large quantities; most of this is temporarily stored in the Cardiff Railway's East Moors Sidings.

The Queen Alexandra Dock, with a water area of 52 acres, was opened on 13 July 1907 by His Late Majesty King Edward VII. This dock, which was rendered necessary by the rapidly growing trade of the Cardiff Docks, is the largest of the five basins comprising the Bute Docks and provides, in fact, nearly one-third of the total water space available. The Queen Alexandra Dock was promoted, designed and constructed under the supervision of the Managing Director of the Cardiff Railway, Sir William Thomas Lewis, Bart.

●

The only tunnel on this line is 325 feet long, and is situated at Castell Coch. The tunnel is succeeded by a cutting of an average depth of 50 feet, and here are two overbridges, one of which has its eastern abutment springing from the rock. At Nantgarw is the severest piece of work on the line; here the canal has three locks, and to hold it up there has been built a retaining wall 427 feet long. The railway next crosses the Merthyr Road by a skew bridge at an angle of 13¾ degrees. South of Treforest the River Taff is crossed by the Treforest Viaduct; this viaduct is 457 feet long between the parapets, and the rails are 55 feet above the bed of the river. The line is doubled throughout, with four lines through some of the stations. The gradients are easy, and generally with the load. Two contracts were let for the construction of the line, the first to Messrs Monk & Newell of Liverpool,

During the trial run of the newly purchased steam railcar on 27 February 1911, seen here at the up platform at Whitchurch station, its distinguished group of Cardiff Railway Company passengers are photographed for posterity. From left to right they are **Mr H. S. C. Ree, Chief Engineer; Mr H. A. Hart, Mechanical Engineer; Mr J. Dudley Stuart, Assistant Engineer; Mr H. E. Allen, Resident Engineer, Construction Works; Mr W. J. Holloway, Traffic Superintendent; Mr W. Lewis Harris, Solicitor; Chief Inspector E. Wilcox; Mr C. S. Denniss, General Manager; The Marquis of Bute; and Sir William T. Lewis, Bart, KCVO, Managing Director.** *The Railway & Travel Monthly magazine, April 1911*

for the length from the Heath to Tongwynlais, which included exchange sidings at Heath and a shunting neck, 900 feet long, running parallel with the Rhymney Railway near the filter beds of the Cardiff Corporation. In this contract there were four cuttings, from which 622,340 cubic yards of material were removed. Contract No 2, for the remaining section, which was somewhat delayed, principally owing to the death of the late Marquis of Bute, was let to Messrs T. Oliver & Sons, of Westminster, and proved to be a much greater undertaking, some 917,000 cubic yards of filling being required, while 11 cuttings had to be negotiated. Taking into consideration the many difficulties to be contended with, it is not surprising that an eminent railway engineer described it as one of the most interesting bits of engineering he has ever seen.

•

The line was finished a year or two ago, but owing to various difficulties, which need not now be gone into, delay occurred to its being opened for traffic, but in the summer of 1910 the construction of the passenger and goods stations was put in hand and orders given for the construction of railmotors for working the passenger services. The engineering strike at the commencement of the winter delayed the delivery of the locomotives, or the line would have been opened some four months ago. A preliminary trip over the line was made on 27 February when the Marquis of Bute started the railmotor car on the new railway, amongst congratulations and a fusillade of fog signals. The Marquis also

drove the locomotive of the mineral train that passed over the railway when the permanent way was completed in May 1909.

The public opening of the railway took place on 1 March [1911], the first train leaving the Cardiff Station of the Rhymney Railway at 9.55am. Among those travelling by the train were Mr C. S. Denniss (the General Manager), Captain T. N. Rosser (the Dock Master). Mr W. J. Holloway (Traffic Superintendent), Mr G. W. Howard (General Manager of the Gloucester Carriage & Wagon Works, the builders of the passenger motorcars), Mr E. A. Prosser (General Manager, Rhymney Railway), Mr A. E. Caswell (of the General Manager's office), and Mr Richard Thomas (Berthing Master), the oldest employee in the service of the Cardiff Railway. The train carried 12 first class and 33 third class passengers from Cardiff. At the various stations en route more passengers joined, and the appearance of the first train was hailed with delight by the folk assembled at the different stations and halts. Rhyd-y-felin, the terminal station, was reached at 10.30 and here again a crowd had collected and cheered the train. The first passenger to purchase a ticket was a lady, who pleaded hard to be allowed to retain it as an interesting memento, but the Cardiff Railway Company exercised its right to collect the ticket, which has since found its way to Cardiff Castle, and a place there amongst the curiosities in the possession of the Marquis of Bute.

On the return journey in a special saloon, the toast of "Success to the Cardiff Railway Company" was proposed by Mr G. W.

Howard, and suitably responded to by Mr C. S. Denniss, who thanked them for their good wishes in this new project, which had presented so many difficulties in its inception and development. The sun was shining upon them that day, and he hoped it was a good augury, not only for the company, but also for the trade and commerce of Cardiff and the colliery district of the neighbourhood. He was glad to see among them Mr Thomas Taylor, who was sinking the first pit on the side of the Cardiff Extension Railway. Both he and Mr Prosser would welcome big loads of coal from the colliery, and they hoped the opening of the new line would inaugurate a very great development of the district.

•

The signalling on the new line has been carried out by Messrs McKenzie & Holland. The passenger stock consists of two (first and third) composite motor coaches, and two third class trailer coaches. These railmotor coaches and trailing cars are supplied by the Gloucester Railway Carriage & Wagon Co Ltd to the Cardiff Railway for working the passenger service over the new line. The motor coaches are constructed with a self-contained engine, which forms the leading bogie, the vertical boiler being fixed at the bogie centre. The wheels of this bogie are coupled, and at this end the vehicle is carried on the "Dean" principle of scroll irons and cross suspension bars. All the cars are 65 feet 0 inches long over mouldings, 9 feet 0 inches wide, and 8 feet 0 inches high from floor to roof inside. The motor coaches are divided into first and third compartments, separated by an entrance vestibule, and are arranged to seat 16 first class and 48 third class passengers. The trailer cars are third class only, but consist of two compartments, separated in the same way as those in the motor coaches. The seating accommodation in this vehicle is for 80 passengers. The car bodies are framed in teak and oak with panels of Honduras mahogany, the roof, floor and interior casings are of yellow pine, and the interior of the roof is lined with three-ply

birchwood panelling. All the interior finishing of the compartments is of polished wainscot oak, the first class seats being trimmed in blue cloth, and the third class seats are framed in teak with pitch pine slats. Passengers enter and leave the cars from level crossings by means of swinging steps controlled from the vestibule by a lever, which folds the steps under an ordinary step board when not in use. Long brass commode handles are attached to these steps, and, being jointed, fold up with them.

The cars are lighted by gas, are provided with steam heaters and a perfect system of ventilation, the air in the vehicles being noticeably fresh and sweet, even when the windows are closed. There is electric communication between the motor end of the rear driving compartment of the motor coach and the trailing car, means being provided for driving from the rear end of each of these vehicles. The exterior of the carriages is painted and varnished, the lower panels being finished in lake, and the upper in light cream colour, the whole representing a very handsome appearance. All the work has been carried out under the supervision of Mr Henry Ree MInstCE, Engineer to the Cardiff Railway. The Cardiff Railway also possesses 32 locomotives, and 973 goods vehicles. The total length of the dock line in single track (including the sidings) is 126 miles.'

The inaugural train that ran over this new line, on 15 May 1909, was pulled by a TVR Class '04' engine, No 98, hauling 12 coal wagons. These open wagons were full, containing coal from the Bute Colliery at Treherbert (just one of many collieries owned by the fourth Marquis of Bute). Attached behind these coal wagons was a brake-van, and behind that was the TVR Directors' saloon carriage, placed there for the comfort of this distinguished party of officials. At the TVR station at Treforest (where this ceremonial train had stopped to pick up Mr Ammon Beasley, the TVR General Manager) the Marquis joined the footplate crew, ready to travel with them the short distance over the Taff Vale Railway Company lines en route to the crossing onto his own metals

Distance from Wharf Road, East Cardiff Docks, also Mile Post mileage.		STATIONS	Station No.	Gradient 1 in	Time Allowances for Freight Trains. See Page 2. Express Trains. Point to point times.	Allow for Stop.	Allow for Start.	Ordinary Trains. Point to point times.	Allow for Stop.	Allow for Start.	Week Days. B Auto Passenger. arr.	dep.	K Goods. arr.	dep.
3	44	Heath Halt (Low Level)	7656	75 R	....	....	.	....	....	..	—	5 32	—	—
4	48	Phœnix Brick Works	..	L	..	..	..	4	1	1	—	—	6 6	6 16
5	10	Rhiwbina Halt	7666	L	....	....	....	....	....	..	5 35	5 36	—	—
5	41	Whitchurch (Glam.)	7636	L	..	..	..	2	1	1	5 38	5 39	6 20	8 18
5	74	Coryton Halt (Glam.)	7650	L	....	....	....	....	....	..	—	5 41	—	—
6	79	Tongwynlais	7624	L	..	..	..	5	1	1	—	5 44	8 25S	T8 30
—	—	Portobello Quarry	....	....	....	....	....	4	1	1	—	—	—	—
8	60	Glanyllyn	7584	L	..	..	..	2	1	1	—	5 49	8 38S	T8 45
9	47	Nantgarw Halt (Low Level)	7662	660 F	....	....	....	....	....	..	5 51	5 52	D	9
10	6	Nantgarw Colliery	..	L	..	..	.	3	1	1	—	—	—	—
10	77	Upper Boat	7633	200 R	....	....	....	3	1	1	—	5 55	8 56	9‖15
11	71	Rhydyfelin Halt (Low Level)	7669	75 R	..			3	1	....	5 58	—	9‖18	—

Above Goods services and a working of the auto-train, in a timetable of 1928. A. G. *Powell collection*

Below Part of the British Railways passenger timetable for 9 June to 14 September 1958. A. G. *Powell collection*

Table 131

CARDIFF, CORYTON, CAERPHILLY, SENGHENYDD and RHYMNEY

Week Days

Miles from Cardiff (G.)		am	am	am	am	am	am	am	am	am		am	am	am	am	am	am	am	am P	am	am	am
	Cardiff (Bute Road) dep	..	..	..	..	6 23	6 40	6N57	6N57	7 35	..	7 35	..	..	..	8N36	9 3	9 40	9 40	1010	1030	10 48
	" (Queen St.) . arr	....	....	....	....	6 26	6 43	7N 1	7N 1	7 38	....	7 38	....	....	....	8N40	9 6	9 43	9 43	1013	1033	10 51
	Cardiff (General) .. dep	4 45	5 20	5 20	..	6 1	6 31	7 1	7 1	7 31	..	7 31	7 31	8 1	8 1	8 40	9 1	9 31	9 50	10 1	1015	10 31
½	Cardiff (Queen St.) .. dep	5 15	5 40	5 45	6 5	6 35	6 45	7 10	7 35	7 40	....	7 50	8 5	8 15	8 25	8 45	9 15	9 45	9 55	1015	1035	10 55
2¾	Heath Halt (L.L.) .. dep	..	..	5 50	..	..	6 50	..	..	7 45	..	..	8 10	..	8 30	8 50	..	9 50	..	1020	1040	..
4	Birchgrove Halt	....	....	5 54	....	....	6 54	....	....	7 49	....	....	8 14	....	8 34	8 54	....	9 54	....	1024	1044	....
4½	Rhiwbina Halt	..	..	5 56	..	..	6 56	..	..	7 51	..	..	8 16	..	8 36	8 56	..	9 56	..	1026	1046	..
5	Whitchurch (Glam.)	....	....	5 58	....	....	6 58	....	....	7 53	....	....	8 18	....	8 38	8 58	....	9 58	....	1028	1048	....
5½	CorytonHlt (Glm) arr	..	..	6 0	..	..	7 0	..	..	7 55	..	..	8 20	..	8 40	9 0	..	10 0	..	1030	1050	..
3	Heath Halt (H. Level) .. dep	5 20	5 45	....	....	6 40	Stop	....	7 40	....	....	7 55	....	8 20	....	....	9 20	....	10 0	....	....	11 0
4	Llanishen	5 25	5 48	..	6 13	6 43	..	..	7 44	..	..	7 58	..	8 23	..	..	9 23	..	10 3	..	..	11 3
5½	Cefn On Halt	....	....	....	....	6 47	....	....	7 48	....	....	....	....	8 27	....	....	9 27	....	10 7	....	....	11 7
7½	Caerphilly .. .. arr	5 34	5 58	..	6 21	6 52	..	7 25	7 54	..	..	8 6	..	8 32	..	..	9 32	..	10 12	..	..	11 12
	Caerphilly dep		6 5																10 20			....

nearby, reached by crossing over that disputed piece of land via the form of a temporary wooden trestle bridge (removed on 12 October 1909). Altogether this had been a distinguished but very costly occasion, and the Marquis was determined to enjoy this inaugural run. If only he had realised that this was to be the first and only time that his wish would be granted.

The aim of the Cardiff Railway Company was to connect with the TVR at Treforest, but the TVR resisted this incursion onto their territory. Arbitration produced an award that insisted that the Cardiff Railway put down sidings at Treforest, and at the Cardiff Railway board meeting held on 24 February 1911 it was decided that this should be done forthwith, once permission to proceed was given by the Board of Trade Inspector, Lt Colonel E. Druitt. Things started moving and it must have seemed to the Cardiff Railway's board of directors that this long and expensive struggle was over.

However, the Taff Vale Railway (by now joined by the Barry Railway) still objected to this devious plan to rob them of a major share of colliery traffic, so they effectively stopped the Cardiff Railway in its tracks by using blocking tactics, via the Law Courts, to create delay and additional expense to the Cardiff Railway Company. Thus the TVR, through careful and skilful use of counter-objections and appeals, reversed decisions made against them to their advantage.

And so it was that, on 1 March 1911 (St David's Day), the passenger service of 11 trips each way by railmotor to the Rhydyfelin terminus finally started (with five each way on Sundays), but with no through connection allowed. The Cardiff Railway Company's dream of diverting the majority of TVR mineral traffic, and their wealth, was over, and goods traffic was restricted to general traffic at the stations, a developing colliery at Nantgarw (Nantgarw Colliery), a quarry (Portobello Quarry near Glan-y-Llyn), and a brickworks (Phoenix Brickworks at Rhiwbina). This scheme had left the Cardiff Railway Company in deep financial trouble, so much so that it applied to amalgamate with the Rhymney Railway, but this plan was refused by the House of Commons. The TVR offered £5,583,300 for the line, but this offer was turned down, as it was over a million pounds short of its capital value. After a second attempt, the Taff Vale Railway Company withdrew, leaving the Cardiff Railway Company to manage its line as best it could.

●

On 1 January 1922 the Cardiff Railway and its docks were absorbed into the Great Western Railway, which already had the Port Talbot and the Rhondda & Swansea Bay Railways under its control. The GWR moved the locomotive works to Caerphilly in 1926, with all carriage and wagon repair work carried out at Cathays and Barry. The Cardiff Parade Station of the former Rhymney Railway was closed, and its services transferred to the former TVR station at Queen Street, Cardiff, on 16 May 1928.

In 1924 *The Railway Magazine* reported: 'The layout of Cardiff Parade station is rather unusual. The older platform, opened in 1871, consists of the usual two platforms, but a new departure platform was added in 1908. This was placed on the arrival side, as there was no room for it elsewhere. Practically all northbound Rhymney trains use this platform, the older platform being reserved for the Cardiff Railway's railmotors, which have used this station since railmotor services started on 1 March 1911, under an agreement. For Cardiff, this station is a poor one and no one will regret it being closed.'

Today there is still a passenger service between Cardiff and Coryton, but that is all that is left of the former route. Some parts of the trackbed remain between Coryton and the Glamorganshire Canal Nature Reserve, and there are also the impressive abutments next to the River Taff at Rhydyfelin. The remainder of the line has mostly been covered by the development of the A470 trunk road and the expansion of the Treforest Industrial Estate.

Heath Junction

Right Ordnance Survey map of 1922, showing the Cardiff Railway line branching away from the Rhymney Railway line at Heath Junction. At the bottom of the map is part of the TVR Roath Branch line. The memorial to Captain Scott (of Antarctic fame), marked on the map at the foot of The Lake, can still be seen in Roath Park today. *Crown copyright*

Left On 30 May 1955 ex-GWR '5600' Class 0-6-2T No 5615, with a down passenger train heading towards Cardiff on former Rhymney Railway metals, passes Heath Junction and its signal box. No 5615 was built at Swindon Works in 1925, and withdrawn from service in 1963. On the left are the lines of the former Cardiff Railway, which once reached as far as Treforest but today only go to Coryton; on the extreme left can be seen a mixture of carriages and vans occupying Heath Low Level Sidings. This is, one could say, not only the start of the Cardiff Railway's dream but also the start of this story. Over the years the Cardiff Railway became part of the Great Western Railway, then British Railways, then, following privatisation, Valley Lines, Wales & Borders, and today Arriva Trains Wales. *J. and J. Collection*

Below Extract from the British Railways working timetable of passenger and Class 4, 5 and 6 freight trains on Cardiff district branch lines, 9 September 1963 to 14 June 1964. *Author's collection*

Middle On Friday 7 November 1952 former TVR engine No 364 (allocated to Cardiff Cathay shed, 88A) running bunker-first, comes off the Cardiff Railway branch at Heath Junction with the 1.46pm Coryton to Cardiff (Bute Road)

Speed of Trains through Junctions and at other Specified Places—continued

Name of Place	Direction of Train		Miles per hour
	From	To	
Heath Junction and Coryton			
Heath Junction	To and from Branch		20
Heath Junction and Coryton Halt ..	The speed of all Up and Down Trains between Heath Junction and Coryton Halt (inclusive) must not exceed 35 miles per hour and must be further restricted to lower speed as shewn below:—		
Whitchurch (Glam.)	Single Line .. .. Down Line		25

service. Formerly TVR 'A' Class No 129, the locomotive was built at the Vulcan Foundry (works number 3182) in 1916, rebuilt with a GWR tapered boiler in 1926, and finally withdrawn from service in 1957. Of the four carriages the inner two are converted TVR steam railcars. The steam from the hard-working engine hides most of the Heath Junction signal box. To the right are the lines of the former Rhymney Railway, while in the foreground is a typical GWR standard type of lamp hut, introduced around 1910, which would have been used for the storage of various items such as signal lamps, petroleum and paint. These corrugated tin huts measured 6 feet by 6 feet or 8 feet. The arrow-shaped sign alongside the hut bears the words 'Safety points'. *J. and J. Collection*

Bottom left The same train is seen moments later from the High Halt Road bridge. Approaching in the distance is tank loco No 35, the driver easing his train towards the up main line signal while hauling the D8 turn, 'Cardiff Docks to Llanbradach Colliery freight'. This former Rhymney Railway engine was formerly No 39, built by Hudswell Clarke & Co Ltd in 1921 to works number 1431. It retained its Rhymney Railway parallel boiler right up to its withdrawal in 1956. In the far distance is Highfield Road bridge. *J. and J. Collection*

Top right DMU set No C302 passes Heath Junction en route to Cardiff on 28 March 1984. The signal box is still to be seen, and in the far distance is the up platform of Heath (High Level) Halt. Note on the extreme left the miniature live steam running track of the Cardiff Model Railway Society. *British Railways*

Middle right Further alterations to the junction took place at the beginning of 1987, as seen here on 11 January, with the new junction in the distance, and the former trackbed at Heath Junction on the left as a grey scar of levelled ballast. *Author*

Right The remains of the original line near Heath Low Level in March 1985. The new junction had opened four months previously on 19 November 1984. *Author*

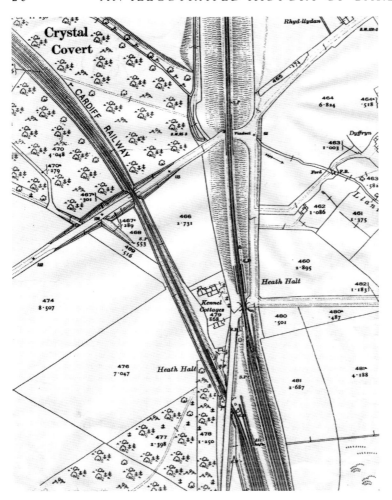

Left Ordnance Survey map of 1920, showing Heath Low Level (left) and High Level Halts. *Crown copyright*

Below Heath Halt, at the commencement of the new railway, had staggered platforms. It opened on 1 March 1911 and the 50-foot-long down platform is seen here in 1920 (with Kennel Cottages behind it); of wooden construction, it appears to have had some of its planks replaced recently, and alongside the pathway is what looks like a GWR 'pagoda' shelter. The view is from Heath Halt Road, which led to Heath Park Avenue and the Three Arches Viaduct on the Rhymney line. The halt was renamed Heath Halt (Low Level) on 1 July 1924 by the GWR and Heath Low Level by British Railways on 5 May 1969, and is still in use today for passenger services. *Lens of Sutton Collection*

Top The platforms were extended in 1930, and this is a view looking towards Heath Junction from the former down platform in about 1960, now being used for traffic in both directions. Almost hidden by the foliage and creeping dog-roses that have spread over the fencing and are creeping towards the line can be seen the canopy of the former GWR shelter and a GWR electric platform lamp. *Lens of Sutton Collection*

Middle Looking towards Ty Glas, this photograph provides a good view of the Low Level halt in the 1930s. Most noticeable are the varied designs of the GWR shelters. On the up platform is a standard type of corrugated tin, which was used both for storage and, as in this case, as a waiting room; this type of shelter would measure either 20 feet or 14 feet by 8 feet. Over on the down platform can be seen the standard wooden type of platform shelter. The chocolate and cream paintwork and wire fencing give a touch of quality to what was initially a low-cost wayside halt. *Lens of Sutton Collection*

Bottom On 25 July 1966 the line was singled from Heath Low Level Halt to just west of the North Road bridge alongside Whitchurch Station. On 13 January 1969 British Rail announced that several South Wales stations would receive grant aid (a conclusion decided upon by BR and the Ministry of Transport); antiquated waiting rooms that had led to a steady increase in vandalism were to be demolished and replaced with modern shelters 'with the provision of facilities for the weather protection of passengers'. The scheme was awarded £120,000; however, costs had reached £150,000 by 1970, and £240,000 by 1973. Of the list of 61 halts and stations, only four from the former Cardiff Railway were included – Birchgrove Halt, Heath Halt (Low Level), Rhiwbina Halt and Whitchurch (Glam) – despite the line running through one of the most populated areas of Cardiff, with a major supermarket (Asda), the M4 motorway and the University of Wales Hospital close by. This March 1985 view shows the new brick-built waiting shelter, open to the elements, with a bench inside. *Author*

Top The short distance between Heath Junction and Heath Low Level Halt was popular with photographers. Seen here is Cardiff Railway 0-6-0 saddle tank No 23 with the 5.22pm passenger train at Heath South on 11 August 1913. Built by the GWR in 1886 to works number 1068, this locomotive was purchased by the Cardiff Railway Company in 1907 to replace the Parfitt & Jenkins-built engine that had been scrapped the year before (also numbered 23). After the takeover by the GWR this engine became No 1676; later rebuilt with a new boiler, it was withdrawn from service in 1926. *LCGB (Ken Nunn Collection)*

Middle In another view taken in the same area, a youngster is caught on film doing what we all have done, looking out from an open window, watching the engine itself bouncing along with the wind throwing smuts and ashes towards face and eyes – an irresistible temptation! This is Cardiff Railway 0-6-0T No 7 with the 1.05pm Cardiff to Rhydyfelin railmotor passenger service on 7 May 1919; the forward-sloping side tanks gave the driver a better view up front when working around the docks on shunting duties. Built by Kitson & Co in 1919 to works number 5182, it replaced Manning Wardle engine No 7, which had been scrapped some three years earlier. Renumbered by the GWR as 685, this engine was removed from service in 1931, sold to a colliery, and finally scrapped, as National Coal Board Grimethorpe Colliery engine No 1, in 1953. *LCGB (Ken Nunn Collection)*

Bottom Approaching Heath Low Level Halt on Sunday 16 May 1954 is ex-GWR engine No 4580 hauling a two-coach Cardiff-Coryton auto-train service; on the left, on the embankment, is the Rhymney Railway line. This '4500' Class engine was built at Swindon Works in 1927 and shedded at the former TVR Cathays shed until withdrawn from service in 1958. On the right are Heath Low Level Sidings, used mainly for the storage of empty coaching stock. *J. and J. Collection*

Above Back in time again, here is another view of Cardiff Railway 0-6-0T No 7, pulling the 2.30pm Cardiff to Rhydyfelin railmotor service on 17 May 1919. Unfortunately the train is hiding a good view of Heath Halt. The bridge in the background carries Heath Halt Road over the line. *LCGB (Ken Nunn Collection)*

Right No 7 is seen again earlier the same day with the 1.52pm Rhydyfelin to Cardiff railmotor service, approaching Heath South Junction. *LCGB (Ken Nunn Collection)*

Right Former TVR 'A' Class No 343 is pulling the 6.00pm Cardiff Bute Road to Coryton service near Heath Low Level on 27 July 1953. Once again the late Sid Rickard has caught the moment superbly as the engine's fireman takes a moment away from his duties to taste a breath of fresh air and check the operation of the injector. This engine, formerly No 11, was built by Hawthorn Leslie & Co Ltd to works number 3060 in 1914; rebuilt with a GWR tapered boiler in 1930, it was withdrawn from service in 1955. *J. and J. Collection*

Above This bridge carries the former Cardiff Railway line midway between Heath Halt and Ty Glas, in line with Heath Way and the rear of the Government offices (on the other side of this bridge). Photographed on Sunday 11 January 1987, at some unknown date the archway of this bridge has been blocked up. *Author*

Below This article appeared in *Model Railway News* in April 1964, written and illustrated by Mr J. R. Bason under the title 'Masonry underbridge, Cardiff Railway'.

NEAR the lower end of the Taff Vale, where the valley floor is wider than the Rhondda Valleys are further north, can be seen the abandoned embankments of the Cardiff Railway. The track and ballast, together with the steel superstructure of the underbridges, have been removed. The drawings give the general proportions of a masonry underbridge which is still standing in a good state of repair.

At this particular location the double track was carried on an embankment, with the rail level about 18 ft above general ground level. The railway crossed a secondary road at right angles. Bridge construction was carried out in a "squared coursed rubble," with the individual blocks being left as "rock-faced"; that is the jointing planes are cut true, with the face of each block being chisled to allow the centre of the face to project about 2 in. from the surface of the block at the joint. "Draughts" are cut on the quoins.

The inside of the parapet and the wing walls were worked to give a reasonably smooth face. For all the remainder of the structure the "rock-faced" surface

of each sandstone block results in a rugged surface. Large capping blocks on the piers have smooth faces on all sides; and the parapet and wing walls are topped with specially shaped blue bricks. The top planes of these uppermost courses are sloped to throw water off towards the outside of the bridge, thus these blocks and bricks form a water-resisting cover to the higher portions of the masonry.

The brick arch ring is of five half-bricks in thickness, and this was employed because a stone ring would have been considerably more expensive to construct. This arch was shaped to form part of a circle, and the leading dimensions were proportioned to suit the conditions of the embankment on each side of the bridge. A "flatter" arch, that is one in which the springing points are placed higher up the structure, would have required a larger volume of masonry in the abutments to prevent the springers from spreading apart under load.

Just above the crown of the arch is one ashlar type of course. This is comprised of blocks sawn

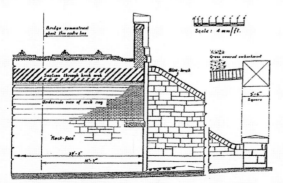

SECTION TAKEN ON CENTRE LINE OF ROAD

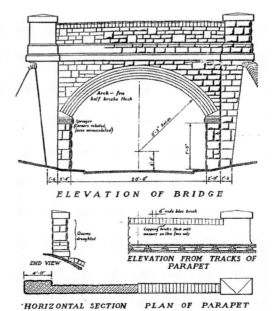

ELEVATION OF BRIDGE

END VIEW

ELEVATION FROM TRACKS OF PARAPET

HORIZONTAL SECTION   PLAN OF PARAPET

Ty Glas

Top A report in the *South Wales Echo* of 20 June 1986 announced good news for people in Llanishen, Cardiff – a new station at Ty Glas would be in operation the following January. It would be served by the majority of trains on the Coryton branch, with both early morning and evening peak services, and from May a half-hourly service would be introduced during the day. The *Western Mail* further reported on 30 September 1986 that the Transport Users Consultative Committee for Wales was delighted with the current trend of co-operation between BR and local councils in setting up new stations, and that in January a £4.8 million investment package for the Cardiff Valleys network would be unveiled by Mid and South Glamorgan County Councils; three of the stations involved – at Fairwater, Danescourt and Ty-Glas – had already been given planning permission. Unfortunately, the station took a little longer, not opening to passenger services until 29 April 1987.

In the first photograph trackside clearing is being undertaken by BR on Sunday 11 January 1987, preparing the site that would eventually become the new Ty Glas station. *Author*

Middle Looking towards Heath Halt, Class 150 'Sprinter' No 150267, on a Penarth to Coryton service, approaches Ty Glas in September 1988. *Author*

Bottom Ty Glas station is seen again, looking towards Birchgrove, on 1 July 1987. In the distance is the A469 Caerphilly Road bridge. *Author*

Above and right This is the stone-built bridge that took the right of way to Ty-Maen, similar to but not quite as rounded as the previous stone bridge. The bridge parapets were topped with good-quality engineering brick, steel blue in colour, and hardened so that no water could penetrate into the bridge structure. These bricks were patterned with a circle of lettering and stamped with the words 'S. J. SAULER JR, TIVIDALE STAFFS'. Where the stamp was applied on a corner the centre of this stamp included three interlocking diamonds. *Author*

Below This is the occupation bridge taking Heol Groes Wen to the towpath of the Glamorganshire Canal, near Upper Boat, as seen in November 1984. *Author*

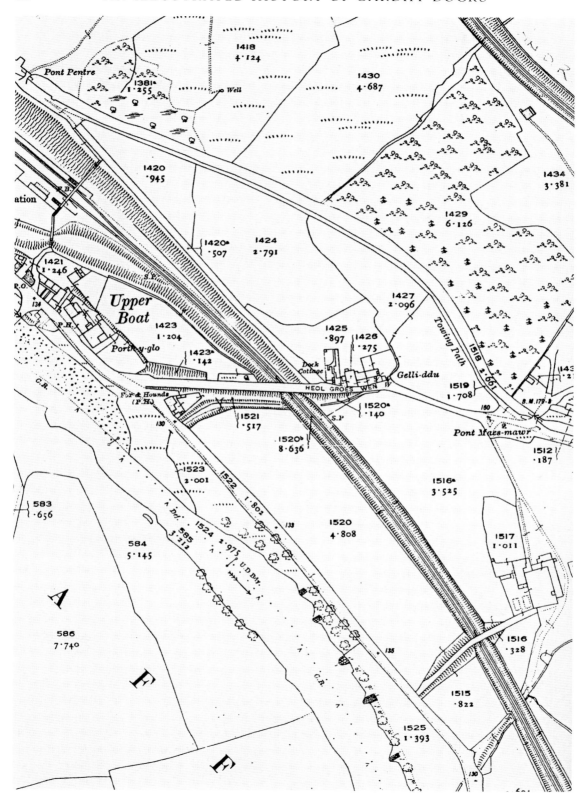

Upper Boat

Left This Ordnance Survey map of 1924 shows Upper Boat station (top left), the Heol Groes Wen occupation bridge illustrated on page 61, Dock Cottage and the nearness of the Glamorganshire Canal; today this canal is but a memory, being covered for most of its length by the A470 trunk Road. *Crown copyright*

Below By 1943 changes have taken place: housing estates are under construction, the former Cardiff Railway line is shown as a 'dismantled railway', and Upper Boat station is 'disused'. In the top right-hand corner of this map is the Pontypridd, Caerphilly & Newport line. *Crown copyright*

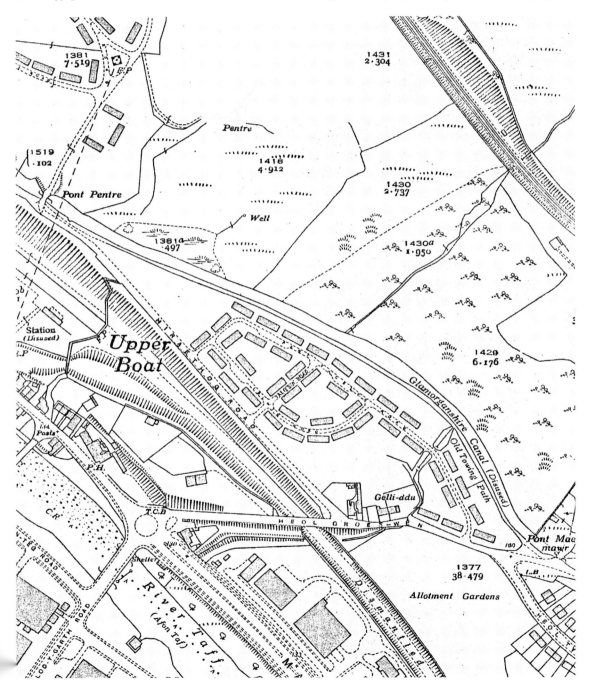

Above Upper Boat station opened on 1 March 1911, its down platform was taken out of use in 1928, and it closed to all services on 20 July 1931. Seen here simmering by the pedestrian footbridge in 1920 is Cardiff Railway engine No 7, later renumbered by the GWR as 685. There are three railwaymen inside the cab – driver, fireman, and possibly a permanent way man. Note the additional coal and the fire irons located on brackets on top of the water tank. Just in view is one of the railcars purchased new in 1911. The footbridge must be one of the longest, linking the platforms with the top of the embankment behind the station and the road in front of it (see the maps on the previous pages). *D. K. Jones collection*

Below With washing on the line and chickens scratching the ground around their hen-house, this is Upper Boat station in 1956. Today the area is the site of a building merchant's premises for DIY enthusiasts. *Lens of Sutton Collection*

This Ordnance Survey map of 1921 shows Upper Boat station and Rhydyfelin Halt (top left), followed by the Cardiff Railway viaduct over the River Taff and the nearby Treforest Tin Plate Works. In the centre of the map are the Taff Vale Railway and Barry Railway lines, also heading for Treforest. *Crown copyright*

Rhydyfelin and Treforest

Council and Cardiff Railway.

The Chairman commented on the fact that the Cardiff Railway Co. had erected their terminus station at Rhydyfelin and said that it would undoubtedly be beneficial both to the railway company and the council's tramway undertaking—if the terminus station was made at the end of New Meadow Terrace, Treforest, which would be about 300 yards walk from the tramway terminus. People from the further end of the town would then probably take car down there and proceed by the new company's train. He moved that the clerk be instructed to write them.

This was agreed to.

From the *Pontypridd Observer*, 8 April 1911. *Pontypridd Library*

Above Rhydyfelin Halt opened on 1 March 1911 as the terminus of the line pending agreement with the Taff Vale Railway regarding access to the TVR line at Treforest. It was renamed by the GWR as Rhydyfelin Low Level Halt on 1 July 1924 and a passing loop and platform were built on the up side in 1928, but the halt closed entirely on 20 July 1931. Here we see one of the newly purchased Cardiff Railway steam railmotors (a composite of 1st and 3rd Class compartments) with the first passenger service to run from the station on the opening day. *Pontypridd Library*

Below Rhydyfelin Halt is seen again in June 1922, with its waiting room enclosed within a fence, the gate of which was unlocked by the railmotor guard. 'Somersault' signals were used throughout the line, and also in view is the conical-style water tower. The signal box, which opened in 1909, contained three levers; it closed in March 1931. *D. K. Jones collection*

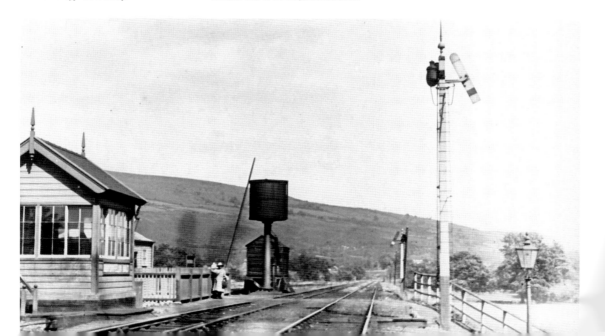

Above The Cardiff Railway's Rhydyfelin Viaduct is seen on 14 October 1933 from the Treforest side of the River Taff, looking towards the Duffryn Arms public house, Duffryn Place and the Cardiff Road. Rhydyfelin Halt is out of sight, but was only a short distance away. The viaduct was 457 feet long from parapet to parapet (other sources give its length as 512 feet), and was supported at a height of 55 feet from the river bed on cylindrical pillars. In 1943 the viaduct was demolished and its ironwork melted down, producing 1,500 tons of scrap to help the war effort. However, the lower sections of the supporting pillars can still be seen, half hidden in the swirling waters of the River Taff. The massive abutments on the Treforest side of the river are still as awesome as ever, and the grass verge from which this photograph was taken is now part of an allotment association. Today only the pedestrian/road bridge is still here. *National Railway Museum*

Below left One of the abutments is seen in August 1986 from the road that skirts the edge of this impressive construction on the Treforest side of the River Taff. *Author*

Below Taken on 29 March 2004 this view shows part of the Treforest Tin Plate Works. Above the centre stones of the two Cardiff Railway arches is a single stone into which has been carved the date '1907'. The viaduct across the River Taff direction is off to the right, and Treforest to the left. *Author*

Left This unusual photograph, initially taken as a record for the Ordnance Survey department, then at Pontypridd, shows the recording of bench marks in connection with Ordnance Survey maps. It was taken at the top of the Cardiff Railway embankment in March 1954, between the River Taff and the former TVR lines at Treforest, and also overlooks the Treforest Tin Plate Works, a site that is scheduled for preservation. In the far distance are the chimneys of the Upper Boat Power Station. *Ordnance Survey Department*

Below Here is another significant photograph, also taken by the Ordnance Survey department in March 1954, showing the arrow marker being used against the post of a Cardiff Railway sign at the very end of the embankment overlooking the area that the railway would have crossed on a gradual downward gradient, had things worked out right for the company. Judging by the nearness of the buildings along the former TVR line, it seems that this was not a case of a bridge too far, but more a case of a very expensive field too far! *Ordnance Survey Department*

Bottom Cardiff Railway drawing No 6549, signed by the engineers, showing the railway's proposed connection at Treforest (bottom left), circa 1908. *C. W. Harris*

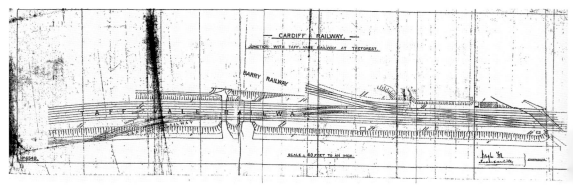

This Ordnance Survey map, of unknown date, was used by the surveyors to mark their recorded spot locations in March 1954. It shows clearly the embankment of the Cardiff Railway in the centre, leading into field number 924c. This was the last piece of ground to be crossed by the Cardiff Railway's short-lived connection with the Taff Vale Railway at Treforest Junction. Unfortunately this field had been purchased in 1898 by the TVR, with the intention of putting their own sidings down, and in doing so they presented a strong case against the Cardiff Railway's traffic crossing it, thus robbing the TVR of a massive amount of future profits;

this was why the TVR had such strong objections to the Cardiff Railway's plans. Some five months after the inaugural train had used the Cardiff Railway junction, it was taken out of use on 12 October 1909 by order of the TVR directors. The line from the south abutment of the Rhydyfelin Viaduct to the edge of the disputed field was closed to traffic on 16 September 1925 and lifted the following year. The railway in the bottom left-hand corner is the Barry Railway's Cadoxton and Trehafod Branch and its Treforest Branch. By now all these lines are owned by the GWR. *Crown copyright*

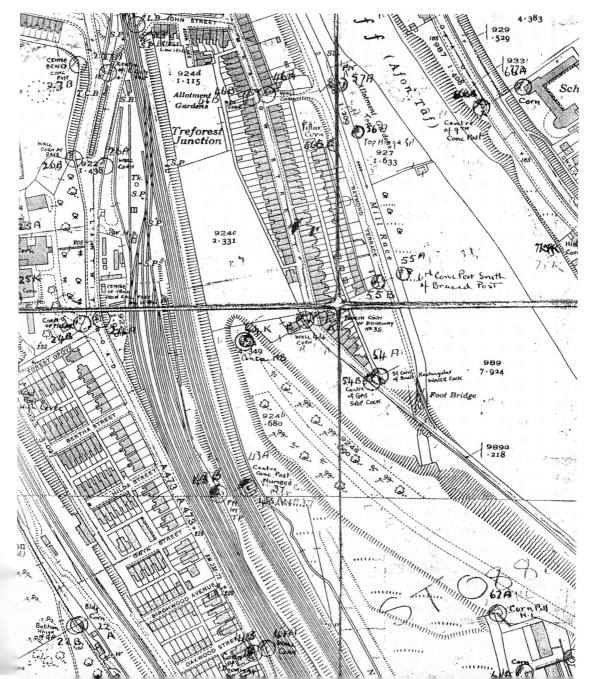

[Ch. cxcv.]   *Cardiff Railway Act,* 1904.   [4 Edw. 7.]

A.D. 1904.

may in making the railway by this Act authorised deviate laterally to any extent not exceeding the limits of deviation shown on the deposited plans.

Power to alter roads temporarily.

8. During the execution of the works by this Act authorised and for the purposes and subject to the provisions of this Act the Company may from time to time alter divert or stop up temporarily any public streets roads bridges and watercourses in any of the lands shown on the deposited plans and specified in the deposited books of reference and any sewers drains gas pipes water pipes and electric or other machinery or apparatus in or under any such public streets roads and bridges doing as little damage as may be and providing substitutes for any sewers drains gas pipes or water pipes or electric or other machinery or apparatus so interfered with and making full compensation to all persons injuriously affected by the exercise of the powers of this section   Provided that the Company shall not alter divert stop up or in any way interfere with any electric or other apparatus of the Postmaster-General except in accordance with and subject to the provisions of the Telegraph Act 1878 Provided also that nothing in this Act shall extend to or authorise any interference with any works of any undertakers within the meaning of the Electric Lighting Acts 1882 and 1888 to which the provisions of section 15 of the former Act apply except in accordance with and subject to the provisions of that section.

For protection of Pontypridd Urban District Council.

9. The following provisions for the protection and benefit of the Pontypridd Urban District Council (in this section called " the council ") shall unless otherwise agreed in writing between the council and the Company have effect (that is to say) :—

The bridges carrying the railway authorised by this Act over Duffryn Road and Ebenezer Street at Rhydfelin in the urban district of Pontypridd shall be constructed as arch or girder bridges at the option of the Company with a clear span of not less than thirty-six feet and with a clear height of not less than fifteen feet from the surface of the roadway but so that if an arch is adopted it shall be sufficient if that height is afforded for a space of ten feet.

Company empowered or may be required to underpin or otherwise

10. And whereas in order to avoid in the execution and maintenance of any works authorised by this Act injury to the houses and buildings within one hundred feet of the railway by this Act authorised it may be necessary to underpin or other-

6

[4 Edw. 7.]   *Cardiff Railway Act,* 1904.   [Ch. cxcv.]

wise strengthen the same   Therefore the Company at their own costs and charges may and if required by the owners or lessees of any such house or building shall subject as hereinafter provided underpin or otherwise strengthen the same and the following provisions shall have effect (that is to say) :—

A.D. 1904.

strengthen houses near railway.

(1) At least ten days' notice shall unless in case of emergency be given to the owners lessees and occupiers or by the owners or lessees of the house or building so intended or so required to be underpinned or otherwise strengthened :

(2) Each such notice if given by the Company shall be served in manner prescribed by section 19 of the Lands Clauses Consolidation Act 1845 and if given by the owners or lessees of the premises to be underpinned or strengthened shall be sent to the principal office of the Company :

(3) If any owner lessee or occupier of any such house or building or the Company as the case may require shall within seven days after the giving of such notice give a counter-notice in writing that he or they as the case may be disputes the necessity of such underpinning or strengthening the question of the necessity shall be referred to the arbitration of an engineer to be agreed upon or in case of difference appointed at the instance of either party by the Board of Trade :

(4) Such referee shall forthwith upon the application of either party proceed to inspect such house or building and determine the matter referred to him and in the event of his deciding that such underpinning or strengthening is necessary he may and if so required by such owner lessee or occupier shall prescribe the mode in which the same shall be executed and the Company may and shall proceed forthwith so to underpin or strengthen the said house or building :

(5) The Company shall be liable to compensate the owners lessees and occupiers of every such house or building for any inconvenience loss or damage which may result to them by reason of the exercise of the powers granted by this enactment :

A 4   7

Above   Cardiff Railway Act of 1904, making provisions for the bridges carrying the Cardiff Railway line over the area of Duffryn Road and Ebenezer Street, Rhydyfelin. *Associated British Ports*

Below   This photograph, showing the Cardiff Railway viaduct crossing the River Taff at Rhydyfelin, is one of a set issued on 30 November 1941 to Luftwaffe bomber crews for raids on Cardiff Docks and elsewhere in South Wales, and may well have assisted the crews of the bombers that followed the former Cardiff Railway line south on 18 May 1943, passing over Whitchurch, Rhiwbina and Birchgrove villages before bombing Cardiff Docks and the nearby area. *Mid Glamorgan Libraries*

CARDIFF DOCKS: STAFF AND MANAGEMENT

The following extracts are taken from Volume 23 of *The Railway Magazine* (1908):

'The works served by the docks contain a great variety of industries, copper works, wagon building and repairing shops, foundries, paint works, flour mills and biscuit factories, all of which combine to substantiate the claim of Cardiff to be one of the most remarkable examples of industrial development to be found in Europe. True it is that a certain amount of shipping was carried on at Cardiff in the 18th century, but it was not until the second Marquis of Bute constructed the Bute West Dock, with an area of 19½ acres, and opened it in 1839, that the vast potentialities of the place were set in motion. Since when a forward policy has been persistently propagated. The second Marquis of Bute died in 1848, but his son and successor, the third Marquis of Bute, was unceasing in his efforts to develop the property and the trade of the port. The present and fourth Marquis of Bute (John Crichton-Stuart), was born on 20 June 1881 and succeeded his father in 1900…

To control this vast system of docks and the railways serving them, men of exceptional ability are required, and the Cardiff Railway is fortunate in possessing as Chairman of Directors, a nobleman so energetic and capable as Lord Edmond Bernard Talbot DSO MP. The Managing Director, Sir William Thomas Lewis, Bart, entered the service of the Bute family in 1854, when, at the age of 18, he was

The third Marquis of Bute, who died in August 1899.
Associated British Ports

The fourth Marquis of Bute, 20 June 1881-25 April 1947.
Associated British Ports

Left Sir William Thomas Lewis, Bart, KCVO. *Associated British Ports*

Above The death of James Hurman, reported in *The Railway Magazine* of September 1908. *The Railway Magazine*

appointed Assistant Engineer to the late W. S. Clarke, the then resident engineer and mineral agent of the Bute Estates. In 1855 he travelled to Cardiff on the first train of steam coal raised in the Rhondda Valley. Under Sir William's supervision, the Roath Basin, the Roath Dock, and the new Queen Alexandra Dock have been promoted, designed, and constructed. After half a century of strenuous life, Sir William is regarded as the most representative figure of South Wales industry and commerce…

Mr James Hurman, the Superintendent of the Bute Docks and Cardiff Railway, is a Devonshire man by birth, but as he commenced residence in Cardiff so long ago as 1850, South Wales is clearly entitled to claim him as one of her own. Mr Hurman began railway work in the telegraph department of the Taff Vale Railway, and in the service of that railway rose to be manager, but in 1891 a difference arose between the shareholders and the board of directors, and when the directors retired, Mr Hurman did so too. He then became associated with many undertakings of great commercial importance, until, in 1896, he was appointed Superintendent of the Cardiff Railway. Possibly few railway officers have spent more time than Mr Hurman in Parliamentary

Committee rooms, which is saying a good deal so far as South Wales and its principal railway officers are concerned. Before his connection with the Cardiff Railway, Mr Hurman was for 30 years in close touch with every Parliamentary measure relating to the railways of South Wales and Monmouthshire. Since his accession to his present important position, not a session has gone by without his presence being necessary – and his strenuous efforts also – in connection with proposals of the Cardiff Railway or other South Walian projects claiming the attention of Parliament.'

From the *Railway & Travel Monthly* magazine of April 1911 comes the following extract:

'Colonel Charles Sherwood Denniss, the General Manager of the Cardiff Railway, comes from a railway family, his father having been the Superintendent of the Hull district of the North Eastern Railway. The whole of Colonel Denniss's business life has been spent in railway work. He commenced his business career with the North Eastern Railway at Hull in 1875, and having gained experience of various departments of that line, he joined the Great Western Railway. In 1892 he returned to the North Eastern Railway as

Top Opening the new British Transport Police Station at Cardiff Docks in November 1968 is the then Home Secretary, James Callaghan, MP for Cardiff (and later, in 1976, Prime Minister). From left to right they are Special Constable, British Transport Police Inspector Bromley (resident at Cardiff Docks), a clerk, Mr T. Roberts (Chief Docks Manager), Mr Callaghan, and another British Transport Police Superintendent from Divisional Headquarters. The British Transport Police on duty in dockyards throughout the British Isles were disbanded on 13 April 1985. *Associated British Ports*

Middle and bottom Taking part in the Cardiff Lord Mayor's Parade circa 1968, the British Transport Docks Board's float bears the legend 'Progress and Development' and the dates 1837 and 1968. A Hyster 'Straddle Carrier' leads the way. *Associated British Ports*

Below This photograph was, I believe, taken in the canteen of the Pierhead Building circa 1965, and is commemorating the receiving of a cheque, perhaps for the Dock Ambulance team or some other charitable cause. From left to right are Albert Luxton (General Cargo Manager, Queen Alexandra Dock), David Roberts (Engineering Department), Bill Streeter (General Cargo Manager), and Raymond Wareham (Assistant Docks Manager). I am grateful to Mr Keith Luxton for sharing with me some of his dock history: his father, Albert William Charles Luxton, his grandfather, Albert Charles Luxton, and his aunt, Queenie Luxton, all worked at Cardiff Docks.

Grandfather Albert Charles Luxton married Miss Violet Brooks on Monday 26 December 1904; he was employed as a railwayman with the Cardiff Railway Company. By the time his son Albert was born, on 10 June 1906, he had risen to the position of railway guard, and at the time of his son's marriage in 1936 he had made good progress up the social ladder. Later that year he retired, having by then achieved the rank of Railway Inspector for the Great Western Railway.

When Albert Junior (ie Albert William Charles Luxton) married Miss Elsie Wicks in 1936 he was employed as a warehouseman in the docks. In 1937 his first son Phillip was born, followed two years later in 1939 by his second son, Keith. By then Albert had become a porter, and was a well-liked man, always involved with raising money for charitable causes. He worked on the General Cargo Quay of the Queen Alexandra Dock as General Cargo Manager, right up until his retirement in June 1971. *Keith Luxton*

Bottom Keith Luxton's aunt, Queenie Luxton, was born in 1917, and retired as Secretary to the Commercial Manager, South Wales Ports, at the age 60 in 1977 after 36 years with the Board and its predecessors. Since 1955 she had worked for six Commercial Managers, all of whom were able to meet up again at her retirement presentation to reminisce and wish her well, before the Port Director, Mr John Williams, presented her with a tray. On behalf of the Board, Mr Dixon presented her with a rose bowl, and on behalf of the present and former Commercial Managers, and the many friends and colleagues from the Central Service Departments in Cardiff, and the Docks Manager's offices at Newport and Cardiff, Mr Thomas presented her with a radio.

The photograph shows Queenie receiving her tray from the Port Director, Mr John Williams. From left to right are Ray Wareham (Port Manager, Cardiff), Les Thomas (Port Director's Office, Cardiff), John Williams (Port Director, South Wales), Bill King (Port Manager, Swansea), Queenie Luxton (Secretary to the Port Manager, Cardiff), Vernon Snow (Port Manger, Newport), Muriel Fishlock (Secretary to the Port Director, SW), and Bob Dixon (Port Director's Office, Cardiff). When I visited the Associated British Ports offices in 2007, the older staff had fond memories of Queenie, who was well respected and admired. *Keith Luxton, South Wales Port Magazine, May 1977*

Above right This photograph was taken at the entrance of the Barry Docks HQ circa 1988 during a meeting of Port Engineers from various ports around the country, after a tour of the ABP Barry Docks estate and faculties, before returning to Cardiff. Harold Lloyd, host of the meeting, is in the front row, third from right; the lady in the front row was the Committee Secretary, employed by Associated British Ports, for this special

occasion. Harold Lloyd retired as Engineer, South Wales Ports East, in 1989 after completing 50 years in the docks engineering departments. Each phase of his long career involved marked changes in a constantly evolving industry – steam to electric, water to oil hydraulics, coal to general cargo, carts to forklift trucks. He started in 1939 as office boy in Newport Docks, then in 1940 began an indentured apprenticeship to F. W. Hawksworth, the Chief Engineer of the GWR at Swindon. In 1944 he moved to Caerphilly Loco and Carriage Works (drawing office), Cardiff Docks (drawing office) in 1946, Cardiff Docks, South Wales Ports (Central Office, Assistant Engineer) in 1951, Barry Docks (Engineer) in 1956, Swansea Docks (Engineer) in 1959, Barry Docks (Engineer) in 1965, Cardiff Docks (Engineer) in 1970, Cardiff and Barry Docks (Engineer) in 1983, and Cardiff, Newport and Barry Docks (Engineer) in 1986. Harold retired in 1989. *Harold Lloyd*

Below Dockers at work unloading grapefruit, circa 1985. *Associated British Ports*

THE

AMALGAMATED SOCIETY OF RAILWAY SERVANTS

OF

ENGLAND, IRELAND, SCOTLAND, & WALES.

Head Offices:—72, ACTON STREET, GRAYS INN ROAD, LONDON, W.C.

In reference to your

TELEGRAPHIC ADDRESS: "BEWARE." LONDON.

Cardiff No 4 Branch.

Address *201 Nabella Street*

August 17th 1900

Mr Richard Bell

Dear Sir

I am instructed to send you the following Resolution   Yours Resp

J Edwards

That we the Members of the Cardiff No 4 Branch pledge ourselves to Cease Work at once, should the General Secretary Mr Bell require us to do so, & Should we Cease Work that we again tender our Claim to the Cardiff Railway Company

Above A reply from the Cardiff Railway No 4 branch of the Amalgamated Society of Railway Servants in support of the famous Taff Vale Railway strike of August 1900. *MSS 127, Modern Records Centre, University of Warwick Library*

Right An agreement between the Cardiff Railway Company and its men, dated 3 March 1910. *T. D. Chapman*

East Dock

Cardiff East Dock engine shed, brick-built with eight roads, opened on the former Rhymney Railway site on 19 January 1931. It was designated shed No 48 CED by the GWR, re-coded by British Railways as 88B from 1949 to 1958, then 88L from 1962 until closure in 1963. However, during the construction of the new Canton Diesel Maintenance Depot, Cardiff East Dock shed was again in use for the storage of the still active and much-needed steam engines. The problem was that by now this shed had been sold to the Rover car company as a storage area for its new vehicles from its factory at Pengam Moor, so it was rented back to accommodate the surviving steam engines, such was British Railways' almighty rush to replace steam with diesel. Thus the shed was back in use for a little while longer, re-coded 88A from 1963 to 1965. It finally closed on 2 August 1965.

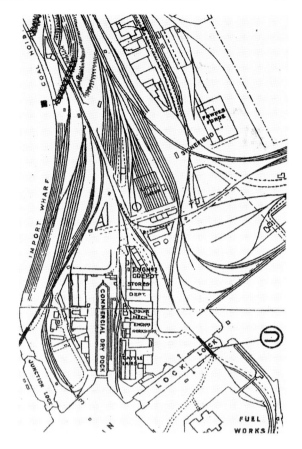

Right This Ordnance Survey map of 1946 shows the layout of the Cardiff East Dock engine shed, in the centre of the map. It also shows the proximity of the Stonefield Yard, while over on the extreme right, above Fownes Forge, is the site of the former East Moors shed. *Crown copyright*

Below Inside East Dock shed in 1953 is former Cardiff Railway No 14, carrying its GWR number 681. Built in 1920 by Hudswell Clarke to works number 1404 as an 0-6-0 saddle tank, it had been rebuilt in 1930 as a pannier tank with a parallel boiler, and was withdrawn in 1955. *D. K. Jones collection*

Left Another internal view, this time on 15 August 1954, shows a line of three saddle tanks. In the centre is GWR No 683, a former Cardiff Railway engine rebuilt as a pannier tank with a parallel boiler in 1926, having originally been 0-6-0ST No 17. It was built by Hudswell Clarke in 1926 to works number 1407, and was withdrawn in 1954. *F. T. Hornby*

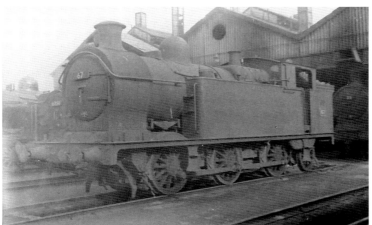

Below left Standing alongside ex-GWR No 6751 on 12 August 1951 is former Rhymney Railway 'A' Class 0-6-2T No 67; formerly No 27, it was also built by Hudswell Clarke to works number 1120 in 1916. It retained its original parallel boiler, and was withdrawn from service in 1952. Behind it in the shed is former TVR engine No 35. *The late G. O. P. Pearce, courtesy of C. L. Caddy collection*

Below Photographed in 1949 is No 5691 in the shed yard next to a varied line-up of coal wagons; the one beside the loco is a GWR steel-sided Loco Coal wagon, and stencilled in the corner is 'Renwick, Wilton & Dobson Ltd, Torquay'. The ex-GWR '5600' Class 0-6-2T was built at Swindon Works in 1927, and withdrawn from service in 1965. *D. K. Jones collection*

Above A good side view of former Rhymney Railway 0-6-2T No 31 (GWR No 77) on 12 August 1951. This 'P' Class engine was built by Hudswell Clarke in 1917 to works number 1121, was rebuilt by the GWR with a tapered boiler in 1929, and withdrawn in 1953. *The late G. O. P. Pearce, courtesy of C. L. Caddy collection*

Below Former Cardiff Railway saddle tank No 32 is seen here in 1953 in its rebuilt form as GWR pannier tank No 684. Beyond is '8100' Class pannier tank No 8457, built in 1950 by the Yorkshire Engine Co Ltd to works number 2450, and withdrawn in 1961. *D. K. Jones collection*

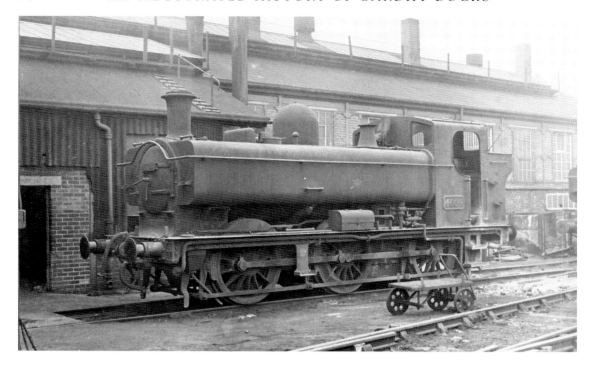

Above Outside East Dock shed on 5 June 1964 is former GWR pannier tank No 4604, built at Swindon Works in 1941 and scrapped in 1965. Alongside is one of the heavy wooden trolleys with cast iron wheels often found around workshops, and used to carry heavy equipment or engine components – but until that missing wheel is found, it is not going anywhere! *D. K. Jones collection*

Below No 681 was formerly Cardiff Railway No 14. Next to it is No 96, formerly Rhymney Railway 'S' Class No 114. Photographed in September 1951, it was withdrawn in 1954. *RAS Publishing*

Right In Cardiff East Dock shed yard, pannier tank No 662 carries the British Railways lion-and-wheel emblem on 5 May 1951; behind is a '6700' Class engine. *R. M. Casserley*

Below right In the centre of this line-up on the same day is 0-6-2T No 155, the former Cardiff Railway No 35, built at Kitson's works in 1908 to works number 4597, rebuilt by the GWR in 1928 with a tapered boiler, and withdrawn in 1953. In front is No 37, the former Rhymney Railway No 41. *R. M. Casserley*

Below The permanent way yard next to the shed was part of the scene, with lines leading to East dock, the engine shed, turntable and coaling stage in an area known as Stonefield Yard. In 1953 we see a line of 0-6-0 pannier tanks. No 682, nearest the camera, was former Cardiff Railway No 16, built by Hudswell Clarke in 1920 to works number 1405; in 1939 it was rebuilt by the GWR as a pannier tank with a parallel boiler, and was withdrawn from service in 1953. *D. K. Jones collection*

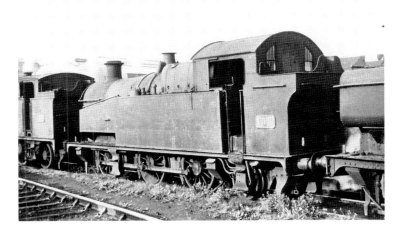

Another view of No 155, simmering away in Stonefield Yard circa 1952. On the left is the mess van for the breakdown crew; the tool van that usually accompanied this van is out of sight. In the distance is a British Railways steel-sided Loco Coal wagon. *D. K. Jones collection*

Page 149

LONG DYKE JUNCTION TO STONEFIELD JUNCTION

Add:

ENGINES FOR EAST DOCK LOCOMOTIVE DEPOT

The Fireman of an engine which has travelled through the section from Tyndall Street Crossing must advise the Signalman at Stonefield Junction by the telephone at the entrance to the depot whether the engine, with tail lamp complete, has arrived clear of the running line.

TRAINS FOR EAST SIDE, EAST DOCK

Trainmen must obtain permission from the Signalman at Stonefield Junction before entering the west side road at the North East end for East side, East Dock.

Telephone communication is available at No. 6 Goods Machine.

Amend heading **STONEFIELD JUNCTION TO RHYMNEY** to: **CARDIFF, QUEEN STREET TO RHYMNEY,** and *delete* complete items:

ENGINES FOR EAST DOCK RUNNING AND MAINTENANCE DEPOT FREIGHT TRAINS TERMINATING AT STONEFIELD JUNCTION

Above An extract from the British Railways Western Region Supplement No 1 to the Working Timetable, Cardiff Traffic District, May 1965. *Author's collection*

Below It is July 1965, and '5600' Class No 5681 is at the end of a line of 'withdrawn from use' engines next to the coaling stage at East Dock shed. This 0-6-2T engine had been built by the GWR at Swindon Works in 1926. *D. K. Jones collection*

CARDIFF DOCKS IN WARTIME

On Sunday 3 September 1939, at 11.15am, Prime Minister Neville Chamberlain announced to the British people that Britain was at war with Germany. German troops had previously entered Poland, then Czechoslovakia and Norway, and in doing so had invoked the treaty that Britain held with those countries. Belgium and France were next to be invaded, so the British Expeditionary Force (BEF) was quickly sent to give assistance. However, the German advance was so rapid that the BEF had to fight numerous rearguard actions to enable its surrounded troops to escape. Mile after mile they fought, holding up the advancing Germans as the British and French troops headed towards an area of beach next to the port of Dunkirk. Six miles inland the British rearguard line stood firm and waited for the advancing Germans. Many thousands of men, wounded, thirsty and hungry, were trapped on the beach; in front of them was the English Channel, behind them their mates holding the line, and a mile from them the enemy. Between 25 and 30 May 1940 the Royal Navy evacuated the waiting men, and by the 30th those naval vessels had taken a pounding; of 41 destroyers, just nine were left, 31 other vessels had been sunk, and 11 were out of action.

Then Hitler made his first mistake: the advance was halted to allow for his supplies to catch up, and the British made good use of their few hours' reprieve. By then 45,000 men had been evacuated, but it was slow work with too few smaller craft available; most men had been evacuated from the 'Mole', the remains of a wooden pier, near Dunkirk Harbour. On 31 May help arrived – hundreds of small craft of every shape and size, Thames barges, trawlers, paddle-steamers, even pleasure craft, all manned by their civilian crews. Picking men out of the shallow water, they ferried back and forth, loading them aboard the naval vessels. Dodging machine-gun bullets and high-explosive bombs

from the constant air bombardment, they battled on. By 4 June 1940 German soldiers were able to walk freely among the sand dunes of Dunkirk. Smoke spiralled upwards from the burned-out vehicles, and the beach was littered with items of equipment and wounded or dying men; 68,000 British troops had been captured or killed, with 40,000 Frenchmen taken into captivity. The operation to rescue the trapped men had lasted ten days, and out of defeat had sprung a victory of sorts, for 750,000 men had been rescued and returned to help defend their country – the

From the *South Wales Echo*, Sunday 3 September 1939. *South Wales Echo/Media Wales Ltd*

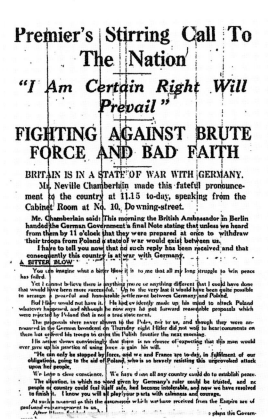

Above This First World War round lapel identification badge was worn by personal working in, or connected with, the Bute Docks under wartime conditions. In this case this badge was worn by Keith Luxton's grandfather, Albert Charles Luxton (see page 78). On the obverse of this enamelled badge is the registered number 1338, and it was manufactured by the firm of J. A. Wylie & Sons of London. *Keith Luxton*

Below This was the Second World War equivalent, Bute Docks now being under the ownership of the Great Western Railway. On the obverse is the registered number J39776, and it was manufactured by Fattorini & Son Ltd of Birmingham. *Author's collection*

beaches closed off to the public, mines were laid where sandcastles once stood; a state of readiness was called for, with blackout curtains fitted and gas masks for civilians issued, carried in cardboard boxes slung over the shoulder by pieces of string. Babies cried when placed in their own full 'baby-sized' gas mask containers. The country waited, and still nothing happened – life went on as usual.

It was when the tattered remnants of the British Expeditionary Force arrived back on these shores from Dunkirk that the 'wake-up call' sounded. On 10 July 1940 the Battle for Britain started. The Germans wanted the South Coast free of air power, which would allow them to land troops on that stretch of coastline. Making use of the captured airfields in France, they could now bomb RAF airfields in this area of Britain, as well as destroying radar stations, thus making detection of the invaders difficult and interception almost impossible. However, the courage of the RAF pilots, mixed with a determination to stop the invasion, took the Luftwaffe pilots by surprise; the flying ability of the RAF's Spitfire and Hurricane squadrons was more than a match for the Messerschmitt Me109 fighters, or the Dornier DO17s, Heinkel 111s and Junkers Ju 88 bombers. However, the RAF was fighting with a five-to-one disadvantage, and this, mixed with a lack of proper sleep, was taking a terrible toll in the loss of aircraft and pilots. Spare parts were becoming scarce, and replacement pilots had insufficient training time. By sheer weight of numbers, airfields were being bombed and Britain was losing ground.

Then Hitler made his second major mistake: he ordered his pilots to change tactics, and bomb towns and cities, as well as the docks and factories that helped the war effort. Thus, on 7 September 1940 the Luftwaffe started its night-bombing campaign. However, for the people of Wales the story had begun earlier, for on 3 July, and again on 7 August, the City of Cardiff and other parts of South Wales were bombed. Further bombing attacks on Cardiff and its docks took place in 1941, when there was eleven, on 2 January, 27 February, 4 March, 12 March, 20 March, 3 April, 12 April, 29 April, 30 April, 4 May and 11 May. In 1942 there were two, on 30 June and 2 July. The last raids occurred in 1943, when again there were only two, on 7 and 18 May.

invasion of France had ended, but the invasion of Britain was about to begin.

From the early part of September 1939 to July 1940 Britain entered a period known as the 'Phoney War', with an expectancy of bombings and invasion. However, nothing happened. The Home Guard trained with broom handles instead of Lee Enfield rifles, wearing a mixture of part issued uniform and part civilian dress. With the

Outbreak of war

Below On Wednesday 20 September 1939, just 17 days into the war, outside the Pierhead Building the Lord Mayor of Cardiff, Alderman W. G. Howells JP, is making a speech before unveiling the commemorative tablet to the centenary of the West Dock, covered by a GWR flag. Although the Government firmly believed that there was a real threat of the Germans using mustard gas, as in the previous war, not one of these civilians has been issued with a gas mask; certainly there is no sign of those cardboard gas mask carrying boxes during this 'Phoney War' period. *Associated British Ports*

Bottom Although the unveiling ceremony went ahead, the proposed celebrations in the city had to be abandoned because of the war. From left to right, the distinguished gentlemen are Sir Henry Nathen Jackson, Bart, CBE; Alderman W. G. Howells JP, Lord Mayor of Cardiff; the Rt Hon Lord Glanely; Councillor George Williams CBE; and Mr W. T. Thomas. The tablet can still be seen on the wall of the Pierhead Building today. *Associated British Ports*

Right The programme for the unveiling. *Associated British Ports*

Below right From the *South Wales Echo*, 4 September 1939. *South Wales Echo/Media Wales Ltd*

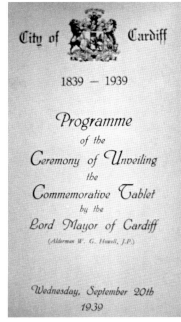

City of Cardiff

1839 — 1939

Programme
of the
Ceremony of Unveiling
the
Commemorative Tablet
by the
Lord Mayor of Cardiff
(Alderman W. G. Howell, J.P.)

Wednesday, September 20th
1939

CARDIFF'S FIRST DOCK

Centenary Celebration Cancelled

CELEBRATIONS arranged for the commemoration of the centenary of the opening of the first dock in Cardiff were cancelled officially to-day.

In view of the impending emergency various functions connected with the celebrations, which were to last from September 17 to 23, were set aside, and the Lord Mayor (Alderman W. G. Howell) decided to-day that it would not be politic to proceed any further with the arrangements.

The only part of the original ceremony that will take place will be the unveiling by the Lord Mayor of the commemoration plaque to be affixed to the outer walls of the offices of the Great Western Railway Company between the West and East Dock basins This is to take place at 11.30 a.m. or Wednesday, September 20, and the ceremony will be of a quiet, informal character. The unveiling ceremony will be performed by the Lord Mayor.

Councillor George Williams chairman of the centenary celebrations committee) said that it had been decided, in view of the circumstances, to cancel the entire programme with the exception of the unveiling ceremony.

"At the same time," he said, "the Lord Mayor and myself wish to express our personal appreciation to all those who have subscribed so generously towards the £1,000 fund, which it was contemplated would be necessary to carry out the various functions arranged in connection with the event."

Above 'Ty Myn Ydd' was situated in the village of Radyr, a short distance from Cardiff, and was the GWR Chief Docks Manager's emergency headquarters during the war. *Associated British Ports*

1940

Below On 20 June 1940, tilted over to port, the SS *Stesso* slowly sinks beneath the water after being hit by a stick of 16 bombs while at anchor in the Bute East Dock. On 9 July 1940 the first fatalities occurred in the docks, when a German bomber dropped a stick of bombs on the SS *San Felipe*, killing seven men. Nine days later, on 18 July, German planes attacked the RAF Station at St Athan. *Associated British Ports*

Right From the *South Wales Echo*, 3 July 1940. *South Wales Echo/Media Wales Ltd*

Opposite middle This wartime photograph shows a cargo of pit props being discharged into open 12-ton coal wagons, some of which are private owner wagons; the vessel is at berth in Queen Alexandra Dock, possibly at King's Wharf. Of the two loaded wagons seen on the 'Water Road' (the one nearest the quayside), one is marked 'Denaby' and belongs to the Denaby and Cadeby Main Collieries, and the other is marked 'Barton'. On

Raider Driven From Wales To-day: No Bombs Fell

The Air Ministry announces that an enemy bomber was shot down by aircraft of the R.A.F. Fighter Command off the East Coast of England early this morning.

A Nazi plane passed over Wales this afternoon. A.A. batteries opened fire, and the plane was driven off flying west. No bombs were dropped. R.A.F. fighters appeared soon afterwards.

R.A.F. fighters also went up to-day when a plane, believed to be German, flew along the South-east Coast some distance out to sea.

Watchers saw the plane flying low in a westerly direction. Ringed by bursting shells, the plane sped seawards and disappeared.

Two bombs were dropped in South-east England. One caused a crater about 5ft. deep and 8ft. in diameter in a road.

The other fell on a common, killing a rabbit, which a man carried away.

Two workmen were slightly grazed by bomb splinters. Other men went on with their work after collecting splinters as souvenirs.

A.A. Guns In Action

The Air Ministry and Ministry of Home Security communique says that several enemy aircraft crossed the south coast this morning and dropped bombs at a number of points. Anti-aircraft defences were in action.

An enemy plane fired bursts of machine-gun bullets off the coast and at soldiers near the beach. Incendiary bombs were also dropped.

Between 20 and 30 high explosive bombs were dropped this morning in a rural area of South-East England. There were no casualties and little material damage is reported, the bombs falling in open country.

One chicken house was damaged at one farm, a number of sheep was reported killed, and at another spot two cows were killed. Between this place and a farm some distance away there were 19 craters.

Planes were heard flying high. Air raid wardens heard the whistle

the next line one of the dock shunting engines stands near two wagons loaded with pit wood; the nearer 13-ton open coal wagon belongs to 'GLM', part of the Powell Duffryn group. The word 'CONTROL' is stamped on the photograph, and many others in this chapter; this is a censorship marking, restricting its use to prevent it being of use to the enemy. *Associated British Ports*

Bottom A decontamination squad is on exercise at the quayside berth of what looks like the east side of East Dock; a proposed mustard gas agent is being neutralised with probably a limewash of sorts, hence the wearing of gas masks. I don't know what the man wielding the sledge hammer is doing! On the right is an eight-plank open coal wagon belonging to Messrs J. & C. King, with an LMS five-plank wagon behind. *Associated British Ports*

Left A pannier tank slowly makes its way around Bute Docks with a rake of tube wagons loaded with degaussing cable. The cable is destined for a ship, within which it will be suspended around the inner hull and attached to a generator. The electric current will then neutralise the magnetic polarity of the ship so that it is not struck by a German underwater 'magnetic mine'. These mines were laid on the seabed and held in place by a magnetically operated release catch; as a vessel passed over them the magnetism of the ship's hull triggered the catch and the released mine rose to the surface and detonated on contact. Note that, with the blackout conditions of wartime, the point levers have been painted white – it was no joke walking into them in the blackness of the night. *Associated British Ports*

Below Under the watchful eye of the tallyman, the end of the degaussing cable is fed through a suspended pulley and hauled aboard by the ship's derrick crane into the hold. On the ship's deck, on the right, is a 'paravane', one of a pair of floats that would be towed on each side of the ship's bow, attached by a long length of wire, their torpedo-like shape easily passing through fairly rough sea. The saw-edged jaws attached to the floats would cut the long mooring cable of any 'contact mine'; these were moored to the seabed and held just below the surface, unseen by passing ships. Cutting the mooring cable allowed the mine to bob up to the surface, where, at a safe distance, a gunshot would detonate it. Later, a similar arrangement, called a 'Side Scan Sonar', used sound waves that penetrated downwards towards the seabed, assisting the Royal Navy in the detection of enemy submarines. *Associated British Ports*

Nine Nazi Planes Down In Channel Fights

6 Dive Bombers And 3 Fighters

Germans Claim To Have Bombed Cardiff Defences

It is officially announced by the Air Ministry that at least six enemy dive bombers and three fighters were shot down over the English Channel in a series of air battles this morning. Two of our pilots are missing.

Earlier the Ministry reported that the battles took place during an attack on shipping.

Despite the fact that practically all the windows and doors were shattered when two bombs dropped near a North Country sanatorium in a raid during the night, not one of the 300 child inmates was injured.

Among other claims made in the German official communique to-day is that A.A. batteries and searchlights at Cardiff were bombed.

News of the battles over the English Channel was first conveyed in an Air Ministry communique issued shortly after noon, which read:

" During an attack on shipping in the Channel this morning a number of engagements took place between our fighters and enemy aircraft.

" Reports so far received show that two enemy bombers are confirmed as having been shot down, and the destruction of several others is reported, but not yet confirmed."

A later communique stated:

" Further reports of this morning's engagements over the Channel confirm that at least six enemy dive bombers and three enemy fighters have been shot down.

" Two of our pilots are missing.

" The above figures include the two enemy bombers already announced this morning."

Story of the Fight

Twelve Hurricane pilots of the R.A.F. Fighter Command lived again over the English Channel this morning an engagement fought by the same squadron more than two months ago in defence of the retreating B.E.F.

To-day, in defence of shipping, the Hurricane squadron took on a formation of about 50 Junkers 87 and Junkers 88 bombers and their escorting fighters. They shot down six of the 87s and three Messerschmitt 109s, as well as damaging others.

Some of Germany's new Heinkel 113 fighters were in action.

Near St. Omer on May 22 there were 10 Hurricanes and 35 Junkers, again with an escort of fighters. In this engagement the squadron shot down six of the Junkers 87, for certain—the same fighter and the same type of aircraft as, to-day—and possibly three more Junkers.

They also destroyed one of the escorting Me. 109 fighters.

Lasted Half an Hour

To-day, as over France, the engagement quickly became a general dog fight, with each of the Hurricane pilots working on his own and attacking bombers and fighters as opportunity offered.

Other British fighters were on patrol at the time near the scene of the action, but made no contact with the enemy.

Left A report of a daytime raid from the *South Wales Echo* of 8 August 1940. Subsequently the Luftwaffe changed tactics to night bombing, and the RAF was quick to take advantage of this. Damaged airfields were repaired and restocked with supplies and spares, and pilots managed to get their first proper sleep for months. Meanwhile, fully trained replacement pilots arrived, replacing those who had been killed or were being held as prisoners of war. However, this reprieve would be paid for with civilian casualties and massive destruction in many cities. The Luftwaffe's fighter planes had only a limited amount of time over Britain due to their fuel capacity, which meant that returning German bombers were without their fighter escorts, so their losses increased. By 31 October 1940 the Battle of Britain was over, but the Luftwaffe raids continued, and for people living in Cardiff and the towns of South Wales the war had only just begun. *South Wales Echo/Media Wales Ltd*

Below An appeal made in 1940 by Lord Beaverbrook, the Air Minister, for aluminium pots and pans to be melted down and turned into Spitfires and Hurricanes produced an incredible response; in addition, iron railings were taken from houses, parks and private estates. More than a million tons of scrap was collected, then came collections of paper, glass and rags, all contributing towards the war effort. The size of this stockpile of scrap at Cardiff Docks indicates the scale of the effort that was made to feed the blast furnaces that would convert the scrap into war material. The scrap would be transported by rail to wherever it was required.

On 13 August 1940 Portmanmoor Road, Enid Street, Eleanor Street and Swansea Street, all close to the Cardiff East Moors Steelworks, were bombed. Later, on 18 and 24 August, RAF St Athan was raided. *Associated British Ports*

KEEP THOSE WAGONS MOVING

Railway wagons are the merchant ships of the land.

Just as steamships bring us warplanes, munitions and food supplies from over the seas, so Railway wagons convey materials of war, coal and the nation's food across the country.

Every wagon held up longer than is necessary is like a ship "laid up" in port.

Every merchant or trader keeping a wagon in his yard a moment longer than is required for loading or unloading is delaying one of the country's overland merchant ships and holding up vital war transport.

1941

The next 15 photographs show the results of one night of bombing. It started on the night of 2 January 1941 and continued into the early hours of the 3rd. High explosive, incendiary and delayed-action bombs rained down on the city centre and the surrounding villages – Grangetown, Butetown, Riverside, Canton, Ely, Ninian Park, Cathay's Park, Llandough (Hospital) and Llandaff Cathedral – as well as the docks. The photographs are all from the archive of Associated British Ports.

Left From the *South Wales Echo,* 3 January 1941. *South Wales Echo/Media Wales Ltd*

Below At the east side of West Dock, on West Wharf Road, heavy bomb and landmine damage occurred between Nos 6 and 7 hoists on the night of 2/3 January 1941. This photograph shows the general view from No 6 hoist. In the centre are the remains of the berthing men's lodges and the traffic men's lodges.

High explosive bomb damage is seen in the area between Roath Basin and Bute East Dock Basin, to the left of the Customs Boarding Station. Of all the varied types of bombs dropped, the delayed-action landmine was the worst. These 2½-ton bombs would be parachuted down and land quietly, while the clock inside them ticked away until the time to detonate came. Some had wires that would be severed by acid eating into them; once parted the explosion would be detonated.

On the right of this view is an engineer's wagon with tool box next to a GWR low-loader against the buffer stops, with nine 'internal use' wood-planked open wagons standing alongside bomb damage created the previous night, which is already under repair. On the left are some open wagons of LMS design, while in the left background is a train of iron-ore hopper wagons. Between the two whitewashed buildings a man on his pushbike heads towards us. The four round-roofed sheds on the right are the N Shed complex, and in the distance can be seen Spillers grain mill and the cranes of Roath Dock. Directly in front of the camera is a First Aid Station.

Bombs have damaged the old stables on West Wharf Road, between hoists Nos 6 and 7.

Left A crater 30 feet wide by 12 feet deep was created by a heavy high-explosive bomb or landmine on West Wharf Road (on the east side of West Dock), damaging the GWR's sewers, lighting and telephone circuits, the old stables and the stableman's house (in the background), and shelter A4, seen on the left. The shelter's roof has lifted and the side wall has been sucked outwards (this sucking out occurred as part of the blast process, similar to seawater drawing away from the shoreline seconds before a tidal wave crashes onto the land). The blast wall at the shelter entrance has been blown against the building.

Left A landmine has damaged the roof and sides of Guest, Keen & Nettlefold's steelworks and the East Dock locomotive shed.

Below The landmine crater can be seen in foreground, while in the background can be seen the damage to the old Fownes Forge building.

Right Bomb damage has occurred at the Albion Works of the Taff Wagon Company near East Dock engine shed.

Right This is Guest, Keen & Nettlefold's steelworks on the opposite side of the road from the Taff Wagon's Albion Works. Firemen are scaling a detachable ladder (probably from a Dennis fire engine) to reach the roof of the GKN building.

Below The same landmine also caused damage to the buildings of the Williams Alexandra Foundry – 'Metal Merchants, Brassfounders ... Pattern Makers', 'Non Ferrous Metal Worked' – opposite GKN. The car parked in front of the coal wagons is an Austin 7.

Above On East Moors Road landmine damage has occurred opposite the British Oxygen Company's premises. A comparatively small crater has damaged the level crossing and a section of rail has been taken out to replace the damaged chairs.

Left Bombs have damaged the roof and walls of the Wagon Repair Shop, also on East Moors Road.

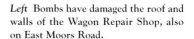

Left Damage was also caused to the Wagon Repair offices; the Repair Shop is in the distance. Two seven-plank coal wagons stand on the left; one is a private owner wagon marked 'Dinnington'.

Above Here is another view of bomb damage to the British Oxygen Company's premises, in front of which is an internal user wagon (former GWR 12-ton wagon No 203204) being used to remove the debris. The 'Beware of Trains' sign is a potent reminder that, no matter how great the damage caused by the bombing, the railway kept on running.

Above right On the night of 3 January 1941 and into the daytime of the 4th the bombs dropped again. A high-explosive bomb has damaged the permanent way and rolling stock in Roath Dock Storage Sidings.

Below Aspects of war from the *South Wales Echo*, February 1941: the theft of a tug, materials for air raid damage repairs, and the death of a GKN employee. *South Wales Echo/Media Wales Ltd*

Relays Of Bombers In Heavy South Wales Raid

FLARES FLOOD-LIGHT COAST TOWN

Nazis Claim Cardiff "Successfully Attacked"

"During last night strong bomber formations successfully raided London and Cardiff. Fires were started in both towns," states to-day's German High Command communique.

Reports from "South Wales Echo" correspondents show that in a heavy raid on a South Wales coastal town a church was destroyed by fire and other fires broke out.

High explosives damaged buildings and houses, and a children's home was hit, but fortunately the inmates had been removed to shelter.

For some hours wave after wave of raiders flew over the town, and at one period so many flares were dropped that the district had the appearance of being floodlit.

Many of the flares were shot out of the sky by tracer bullets from machine-guns.

Casualties were caused in this town and in other South Wales districts where, however, the raids were not so severe.

Raiders were also reported over Southern England and London.

The bombers returned on the night of 26/27 February 1941 in a raid on the docks that injured two firemen of the Auxiliary Fire Service as well as imposing heavy high-explosive damage on the Crown Fuel Company's premises, a gantry, an engine house and stables (which would have housed horses used for everyday hauling duties around the docks, but it is probable that they were empty as by now the docks were mechanised).

Right Business as usual at the Cardiff Stock Exchange, 27 February 1941. *South Wales Echo/Media Wales Ltd*

> **CARDIFF STOCK EXCHANGE**
>
> **Quiet Conditions Ruled**
> (By Our Docks Correspondent)
> Dealing was on a smaller scale on the Cardiff Stock Exchange to-day, but there was very little change to note in the general tone.
> **BUSINESS DONE**
> (Supplied by Cardiff Exchange)
> Conversion Loan 3 per Cent., 101⅞.
> G.W.R. 5 per Cent. Consolidated Pref., 87⅞.
> Southern Deferred: 10½ (twice).
> London County Council 3¼ per Cent. (1958-68), 101⅞.
> Beechams Deferred, 8s 0½d.
> Courtaulds Ordinary, 20s 3d.
> Tate and Lyle Ordinary, 49s 6d.
> Anglo-American Corporation, 31s 6d.
> United African Exploration, 3s 3d.
> West Rand Cons, 31s 0½d.
> **CHANGES IN QUOTATIONS**
> **Rises**
> Distillers Ord. 6d, to 63s
> **Falls**
> Chellew Navigation 6d, to 7s 6d.

Left A report of the raid in the *South Wales Echo* of 27 February 1941. *South Wales Echo/Media Wales Ltd*

Below and opposite page Photographic records of the damage caused during the raid. *Associated British Ports*

CARDIFF CHOSEN FOR LUFTWAFFE'S FIERCEST FIRE RAID

CITY PLASTERED WITH THOUSANDS OF BOMBS

Trail of Reckless Destruction

BOMBER DOWN

"One of the greatest fire raids of the War" was a description applied by public officials to the intensive attack on Cardiff last night.

This morning ruins marked the trail of the night's reckless destruction. Big fires were raging at one time, but early this morning they were all well under control.

Churches, several schools, including two boys' schools, an institute, and some shops were laid waste, and are now a pile of ruins into which weary fire fighters, who have been up all night, continue to pour water.

"I doubt if any town has had more incendiary bombs showered upon it in one raid," said Chief Constable James Wilson. "It was a real pyrotechnic display."

There were a number of casualties, and some people were killed in the raid, which started soon after dusk and continued for some time.

A hospital was busy dealing with air raid casualties when it was itself struck. Operations were in progress at one of its theatres when it was shattered by a bomb, but thanks to the work of the nurses and staff there was not a single casualty. Many patients were evacuated during the night and this morning. They have been distributed to hospitals in the mining valleys.

One of the aircraft which bombed the city was destroyed by A.A. gunfire.

Flares heralded the arrival of the enemy planes, and these were followed quickly by showers of incendiary bombs scattered in many parts of the town from successive waves of aircraft. A persistent barrage kept the enemy machines at a great height. Fire-watchers, street fire parties, A.R.P. workers and the fire brigades tackled the fire bombs with matchless courage, despite the fact that later arrivals of aircraft dropped many high explosive bombs of all calibres, including several delayed action bombs.

RAIDER HIT

Another Roman Catholic church was set alight, but the fire was got quickly under control. A Methodist church, however, was destroyed, and a Welsh church was also razed to the ground. Close by a school was burned out.

People rushed out of their houses when an aeroplane was heard losing height rapidly. This followed a terrific crash in the sky. "The plane came very low indeed and it was easy to tell that it had serious engine trouble," an A.R.P. warden said.

The crippled raider was last seen still losing height, with anti-aircraft shells bursting around it.

CRIPPLED FIRE FIGHTERS

One of the pluckiest bits of fire fighting concerned a business office. The staff voluntary fire watchers were three men of whom only one was really fit. His two companions were men crippled in the last war. One was minus an arm and the other wore an artificial leg.

While the fit man was telephoning from a nearby building a rain of incendiaries broke through the roof of the offices where his colleagues continued their vigil.

Crippled though they were they immediately attacked the bombs with sandbags and extinguished them. The one-armed man made a gallant, but unsuccessful attempt to get a stirrup pump to function. The men were able to keep the flames in check until the arrival of the fire brigade.

Further along the street a Roman Catholic church was penetrated by a number of incendiaries. Walls [...]

BOMBER'S FATE

Parts of the wings of the bomber destroyed at Cardiff last night were picked up on the roofs of houses to-[...]

Above Heavy high-explosive bomb damage to rolling stock and the permanent way was inflicted on Roath Sidings on the night of 3/4 March 1941. This steel-sided Ebbw Vale Colliery wagon has been turned up onto its end door, such was the strength of the explosion. *Associated British Ports*

Below More damage to track and wagons on the east side of Bute East Dock during the same raid. *Associated British Ports*

Left From the *South Wales Echo*, 5 March 1941. *South Wales Echo/Media Wales Ltd*

Right Damage caused during the air raid of 4/5 March 1941 at Roath Dock and the Marshalling Sidings. *All Associated British Ports*

Two Bombers Down In Bristol Channel

Cardiff Again the Main Target of Attack

Nazi bombers visited Cardiff for the second night in succession on Tuesday and their main objective was a residential area, where damage was done to churches, schools, the public baths and library, and a number of houses.

It is officially announced that an enemy bomber was shot down into the Bristol Channel during the night. A member of the crew who baled out was dead when picked up.

It is reported that a second 'plane was brought down, also in the Bristol Channel, and two enemy aircraft were heard in difficulties off a South Coast of England town, where naval guns added to the heavy A.A. fire against 'planes thought to be attacking shipping in the English Channel.

The Air Ministry and Ministry of Home Security communique states:

Enemy activity last night was again not on a large scale. It was confined to the southern part of the country and ceased about midnight.

The main target was one district in South Wales, where some fires were caused, but most of them were soon extinguished, and all were under control in the course of the night.

Elsewhere a small number of bombs were dropped, mainly on the South Coast and near the Thames Estuary, but no important attack developed anywhere, and little damage was done.

Casualties during the night were small.

Giving news of last night's air attacks on Great Britain the official German News Agency says. "Several German bombers attacked Southampton on Tuesday night and scored effective hits on the harbour works. Last night's attack on Cardiff lasted several hours. In at attack on London Tilbury Docks were bombed."

The official German News Agency admits that one German 'plane was lost during last night's raids on Britain. It states that no R.A.F. 'planes were over Germany or German occupied territory during the night.

A delayed-action bomb has damaged Marshalling Siding No 12 during the raid of 4/5 March, and permanent way gangs are working hard to clear the mess of twisted track. Damaged Ebbw Vale wagons have fallen into the bomb crater, but the scene will be back to normal before the gangers leave. However, bearing in mind that delayed-action bombs caused this, there was always doubt in the minds of the men that one had yet to go off; such bombs were as much psychological as they were deadly. *Associated British Ports*

Above Another view of Marshalling Siding No 12 following the same raid, where a selection of private owner wagons have been damaged. On the left is a Thomas & Co Ltd wagon, then one belonging to Bolsover – this is a standard 1923-design, seven-plank 12-ton wagon, with a livery of red oxide with white lettering, registered with the LMS and LNER. *Associated British Ports*

Left Railways weren't the only transport network to be affected by the war. From the *South Wales Echo*, 13 March 1941. *South Wales Echo/Media Wales Ltd*

Below The Docks' First Aid Squad are carrying out an anti-gas exercise, circa 1941, at the cattle lairage, Roath Dock. They are wearing full protective clothing, rubberised raincoats, Wellington boots, rubber gloves, tin helmets, gas masks, and canvas gasmask holders slung over their shoulders. *Associated British Ports*

"FULL UP!"

That is the greeting workers sometimes receive at boarding points on our services when going to and from their jobs.

If your time is your own, it is up to you to avoid travelling during "rush" hours, and so give the workers room on the buses.

To those who are considerate we say "Thank you." To the not-so-considerate we make a further appeal to regulate their travel to more suitable times.

WESTERN WELSH
OMNIBUS COMPANY, ELY.

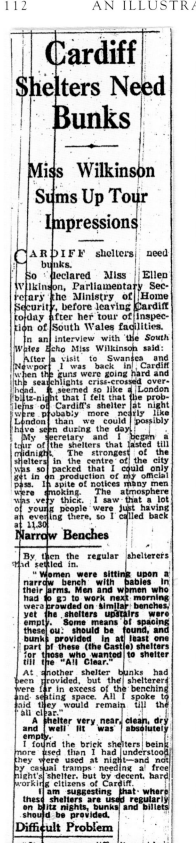

Cardiff Shelters Need Bunks

Miss Wilkinson Sums Up Tour Impressions

CARDIFF shelters need bunks.

So declared Miss Ellen Wilkinson, Parliamentary Secretary the Ministry of Home Security, before leaving Cardiff to-day after her tour of inspection of South Wales facilities.

In an interview with the South Wales Echo Miss Wilkinson said:

After a visit to Swansea and Newport I was back in Cardiff when the guns were going hard and the searchlights criss-crossed overhead. It seemed so like a London blitz-night that I felt that the problems of Cardiff's shelter at night were probably more nearly like London than we could possibly have seen during the day.

My secretary and I began a tour of the shelters that lasted till midnight. The strongest of the shelters in the centre of the city was so packed that I could only get in on production of my official pass. In spite of notices many men were smoking. The atmosphere was very thick. I saw that a lot of young people were just having an evening there, so I called back at 11.30.

Narrow Benches

By then the regular shelterers had settled in.

"Women were sitting upon a narrow bench with babies in their arms. Men and women who had to go to work next morning were crowded on similar benches, yet the shelters upstairs were empty. Some means of spacing these out should be found, and bunks provided in at least one part of these (the Castle) shelters for those who wanted to shelter till the "All Clear."

At another shelter bunks had been provided, but the shelterers were far in excess of the benching and seating space. All I spoke to said they would remain till the 'all clear.'

A shelter very near, clean, dry and well lit was absolutely empty.

I found the brick shelters being more used than I had understood they were used at night—and not by casual tramps needing a free night's shelter, but by decent, hard working citizens of Cardiff.

I am suggesting that where these shelters are used regularly on blitz nights, bunks and billets should be provided.

Difficult Problem

Anderson shelters

On the variety stage and on the radio jokes were made about them and families used them as a place for disused items, but these tin sheds had come to stay. Once erected there is no doubt that the civilian population were dubious as to what protection would be offered by these covered dugouts in their back gardens, as against staying in the house. This was the state of mind during the 'Phoney War' period, when ordinary people had their first encounter with what was officially known as the Galvanised Corrugated Steel Shelter, otherwise known as the 'Anderson shelter'.

In late 1939 the *Great Western Railway Magazine* featured an article on the 'Distribution of Air Raid Shelters', from an interview with Mr D. Hawkeswood:

'The whole of the components have to be properly assembled, into complete sets of parts, before delivery is effected. This work the railway companies are doing. The initial order was for 400,000 shelters, or approximately 180,000 tons of steelwork, to be produced by the manufacturers in 13 weeks, 19 firms are making the steel sheets, 38 more constructing the angles, tees and channels, and a further 21 the bolts, nuts, etc.

Two-thirds of the sheet manufacturers are situated in South Wales and Monmouthshire, so that the Great Western Railway

Left From the *South Wales Echo, 15 March 1941. South Wales Echo/Media Wales Ltd*

Left South Wales Echo, 30 April 1941. South Wales Echo/Media Wales Ltd

PUBLIC NOTICES

CITY OF CARDIFF.

DOMESTIC AIR RAID SHELTERS.

The Income limit for householders eligible for free shelter has now been increased to £350 per annum, plus £50 for each child in excess of two, who is below school leaving age.

Persons not already provided with shelter who are within the above income limit are invited to obtain an Application Form from the City Engineer's Department, City-hall, or 107, Richmond-road.

In suitable cases, applicants may be offered a steel Indoor Shelter of table shape, 6' 6" long by 4' 0" wide—a sample of which may be seen at 107, Richmond-road.

Such shelters are capable of accommodating single households not exceeding two adults and 1 older child (or two younger children) and they may only be erected on the lowest floor of a building not more than three storeys high.

SALE OF SHELTERS.

Householders whose income exceeds the above limit may make application on the appropriate form to purchase an Indoor Shelter for cash payment of £7, 13, 6, delivered.

D. KENYON REES,
Town Clerk and A.R.P. Controller.
City-hall, Cardiff.
April 1941.   a671

Right South Wales Echo, 3 May 1941. South Wales Echo/Media Wales Ltd

£18,000 A MONTH

Cost of New Cardiff Scheme

Cardiff has been asked by the Government to spend £18,000 a month, to be provided by grant, on an extended air-raid shelter programme.

This was disclosed at a meeting of the A.R.P. committee on Friday when the city engineer (Mr. G. H. Whitaker) said that it was proposed that the grant would be operative for six months. That meant that the Government had placed £108,000 at Cardiff's disposal for making waterproof existing Anderson shelters and providing new surface shelters in residential areas. Approximately 500 men would be employed on the work every week.

Company is vitally concerned in a huge proportion of the traffic.

The steel sheets were regarded as the "key" parts, and having regard to the huge number involved, it was first essential to give careful attention to their loading in rail wagons. The plan evolved provided for complete sets of sheets, for every 150 shelters, to be loaded into six wagons, "A"-type sheets in three wagons, "B"-type in one wagon, "E"-type in one wagon, and "C," "D" and "F"-type sheets in one wagon. The other component parts presented no great difficulty, but as the sheets were to be constructed by sheet manufacturers, and the channels, tees and angles separately by the heavy steel manufacturers, and the nuts, bolts, etc, by firms specialising in such manufacture, it will be gathered that no less than five firms were engaged in producing the various parts necessary for each shelter. It was essential for the arrival of the various sections at destination stations to synchronise as nearly as possible on the same day, in order that there should be no interruption in the delivery schedules.

This was accomplished by the setting up of an allocation committee comprising of representatives of the Home Office, the Sheet Makers Association, sections of the British Iron and Steel Corporations and the Railway Companies, meeting weekly at the offices of the Iron and Steel Federation, Steel House, Tothill Street, Westminster, to agree the allocation to each area in the country. Over 1,000 wagon loads of steel sheets are now being despatched weekly from Great Western Railway stations in South Wales to destinations in the London area. In the Birmingham district, Kent, Portsmouth, Southampton and other places, as previously mentioned, the railway companies were asked to undertake the task of delivering the shelters to the addresses notified by the Home Office, and it was agreed that each shelter would be delivered complete. It was necessary, therefore, to consider a plan for loading all the component parts of the shelter on road vehicles at the goods stations, in order that each householder should receive only one call. The carmen have instructions to deliver shelters to the exact position in each back garden required by the householder. Here the size of the curved sheets, in relation to the very limited space available in the halls and passageways of the small houses, presented, as may well be imagined, many and varied problems. Only a proportion of the houses have side or back entrances, and deliveries have mainly to be effected through the front door. This has necessitated removing pictures from walls, hat and umbrella stands, and even, in some cases, the gas brackets. It is pleasing to record, therefore, that there have been few, if any, damages to property. Deliveries are being effected from the following stations on the Great Western system; the total number of shelters are now averaging 6,000 per week, from Paddington, Tyseley, South Lambeth, Soho & Winson Green, Bristol, Small Heath, Cardiff and Plymouth…'

These Anderson shelters would be made as homely as possible by the householders to whom they were allotted, but they were cold at night, damp, and offered little protection from a near miss. Usually they consisted of whatever comforts could be put into them. A stove was a luxury, as were bunk beds; more than likely you had a blanket wrapped around you, and a candle placed under an up-turned clay plant pot, giving just enough heat to take the chill out of the air, until the neighbours popped in for a chat, or to borrow some of your tea or sugar ration.

The other shelter was the Morrison type, a steel cage that would be placed under a table, and into which you crawled for protection (similar to the underwater cages that photographers use when photographing sharks, and with just about the same level of safety!). No wonder people hid under the stairs, or used the cellar if they had one. However, no matter what cover you had a direct hit killed you; a near miss could mean being buried alive and hoping for rescue, if the gas escaping from broken gas pipes didn't get to you first…

More than 20,000 shelters were allotted to the residents of Cardiff. At the end of the war 600 homes had been destroyed, with another 30,000 damaged.

INDUSTRIAL REGISTRATION 1941 (No. 1)

ORDER

Men who have worked in shipyards must register

Men aged 20 or over who have worked for 12 months in any one of the underlisted trades since March, 1926, are required to register at their local Employment Exchange between **Mon. 17th March and Wed. 19th March** (from 9 a.m. to 4 p.m.). The only exceptions are men who on 24th February, 1941, were employed on shipbuilding or ship-repairing (including marine engineering where this is carried on in a shipbuilding or shiprepairing establishment). Men who are not able to call at the Employment Exchange during the times stated should write to the nearest Local Office of the Ministry of Labour and National Service for a form by which they can register by post. All enquiries should be made to the nearest Local Office of the Ministry of Labour and National Service.

LIST OF OCCUPATIONS

Angle Iron Smith, Angle Iron Smith's Striker or Hammerman
Blacksmith (Ship), Blacksmith's Striker or Finisher (Ship)
Boilermaker (Ship)
Boiler Fitter or Mounter, Boiler Pipe or Tube Fitter or Expander, Boiler Coverer, Boiler Scaler (Ship)
Carpenter, Concreter (Shipyard)
Coppersmith (Shipyard)
Craneman (Shipyard)
Draughtsman (Ship)
Driller, Countersinker (Machine or Hand) (Ship)
Electrician (Ship), Wireman (Ship), Electrician's Labourer (Ship)
Fitter (Ship), Fitter's Labourer (Ship)
Iron Caulker, Tank Tester, Felter or Packer

Painter (Ship), Red Leader, Scaler
Plater, Slipper
Plater's Helper (Ship)
Plumber (Ship), Plumber's Mate (Ship)
Rigger, Sailorman
Riveter, Holder-up, Bumper-up, Rivet Heater
Sheet Metal Worker (Shipyard), Sheet Iron Worker (Shipyard)
Ship Joiner, Ship Carpenter
Shipwright, Boat, Barge or Yacht Builder, Boatwright, Block or Spar Maker, Loftsman, Liner-off, Shipwright's Labourer
Stager
Timekeeper, Piece Work Counter, Wages Clerk (Shipyard)
Welder (Electric) (Ship), Burner, Cutter

★ as announced by the B.B.C.

ISSUED BY THE MINISTRY OF LABOUR & NATIONAL SERVICE

Left and below Extracts from the *South Wales Echo* of 17 March (*left*) and 13 March 1941. *South Wales Echo/Media Wales Ltd*

Bombs on Wales

Bombs fell at five places in Wales; three in the South and two in the North, but little damage was done and casualties were few.

Two people were killed and four or five injured when a shelter was hit in a South Wales town, and elsewhere a public-house was damaged and some houses struck.

To-day's German High Command communique states:—

"Throughout the whole of last night which was moonlit and of good visibility, several hundred German bombers in a series of waves attacked the harbour works of Liverpool and Birkenhead with very great success."

Below Outside No 1 Shed, Queen Alexandra Dock, circa 1941, cranes are discharging cargo from the SS *Suffolk*. On the Water Road under the legs of cranes Nos 7, 9 and 11 are a mixture of sheeted and unsheeted wagons belonging to the LMS and LNER. A docker is walking along No 2 road; the van on the left on No 1 road may be a GWR insulated van, and to its left a flatbed wagon is on the Stage Road (the one next to the loading bay). In the foreground are a set of 'paravanes', destined to be loaded aboard a vessel where they will be towed from the bow, the vanes regulating their depth and their saw-edged jaws cutting the mooring cables of any submerged 'contact mines'. *Associated British Ports*

Above Porters are hard at work transferring frozen meat from railway vans onto trolleys and into the Cold Store at King's Wharf, circa 1941. This is New Zealand lamb, and in those days of coupons and ration books, when a housewife would queue for hours to collect a meagre allowance of mince or some sort of sausage, this meat on these trolleys must have been a temptation – but the men also knew what it cost in lives to bring it here. *Associated British Ports*

Left South Wales Echo, 28 March 1941. *South Wales Echo/Media Wales Ltd*

Right South Wales Echo, 27 March 1941. *South Wales Echo/Media Wales Ltd*

Below Inside the King's Wharf Cold Store the lamb is stacked in one of the storage compartments, which were served by lifts. *Associated British Ports*

Above Cable-layer LC20 is in the Inner Lock of Bute East Dock, just before entering the dock itself. The bow suggests that she has at one time been engaged on in-shore submarine cable-laying or carried out repairs to them; however, the side fenders suggest that she may have been laying pipework for land drainage or for sewage outfalls around the coast. The building in the background is the Bute Dry Dock offices, the name of which has been blackened out for security reasons. *Associated British Ports*

Below This is one of the many mass-produced 'Liberty' ships having her cargo of timber discharged at the General Cargo berth on the north side of Roath Dock; N Shed can be seen in the background. Above the ship's stern gun flies the British Merchant Navy flag, the 'Red Duster'. On the quayside is a varied selection of wagons, including a GLM private owner coal wagon. *Associated British Ports*

Country's "Crying Need For Coal"

"Evans of the Broke"

"FOR the next four months I want a pick-and-shovel blitzkrieg to help beat that —— Hitler."

These were the words with which Admiral Sir Edward Evans ("Evans of the Broke") vigorously summed up his appeal in Cardiff to-day to Welsh miners to turn out every possible ton of coal to help Britain to victory.

Admiral Evans, who is a Regional Commissioner in London, is touring the coalfields for the Government, to tell the miners the country's crying need for more and more coal.

He has personal associations with Wales, and he told the delegates how he used to go down the boiler-room of his ship and shovel coal himself so as to relieve the stokers.

Recalling the days when he sailed with Scott from Cardiff on the South Pole expedition, he told of the heroism of the Cardiff sailor, the late Bill Lashley, who towed him a hundred miles across the ice fields when he was down with scurvy.

Forbears from Cardiff

"My forbears came from Cardiff," he said. "My great-grandfather was a miner, and he could sling it across! He had a row with the foreman, and then he walked from the Rhondda to Lancashire, where he started again as a miner. He became the manager; then managing director, and then bought out all the other directors, and he made a devil of a lot of money out of it, because he knew the miner and could play fair all round."

Admiral Evans said that he was carrying the Prime Minister's message to the miners which was that immediate increase in coal output was vital to the Forces and to the industries which were supplying the weapons.

"Immediate increase in output very nearly means victory," he said. "Britain is fighting with her back to the wall. She is facing the gravest hour in her history, and it is really a race against time."

Secretary for Mines

The Secretary for Mines, Mr. D. R. Grenfell, was also present, and said that the slogan for to-day was, "Workers of the world unite lest stronger chains than ever be forged to bind you into perpetual slavery."

Mr. James Griffiths, M.P., said that the nation could not get its vital necessities without coal.

"The nation is finding that out now," he said. "I hope that the nation will not forget it." (Loud applause). We may be beaten because we allowed mines and miners to go to rust!"

Mr. Arthur Horner, president of the S.W.M.F., closing the public part of the conference, said, "South Wales miners, given a square deal, will give the country all that is being asked for."

Above To deal with emergencies that might arise during the war, the Ministry of Shipping erected three large warehouses, Nos 1, 2 and 3, for its own use. No 1 Shed was of brick construction with a single floor measuring 602 by 203 feet wide; it was located on the north side of Queen Alexandra Dock, at the Import Wharf. After the war it was renamed A Shed. Behind it was No 2 Shed, another brick construction measuring 441 by 123 feet; this was later renamed B Shed. To the left of No 2 Shed was No 3 Shed, again of brick and measuring 722 by 144 feet and later renamed C Shed. All three were intended for the storage of grain and general cargo, but as the war progressed they stored many varied commodities.

In June 1941 a dockers' canteen was established in No 1/A Shed. Any place to sit down and take a look at the daily paper, and have a cuppa and a quiet fag, was welcome, although it is almost empty here. It was rough and ready, with trestle tables and wooden benches, but there seem to be plenty of salt and pepper pots around – to these men and many others it was luxury. On the wooden partition behind the distant serving area is chalked 'Canteen open 8.30am' The closing time is unfortunately unreadable. Another chalked message on the right reads, 'Pleases bring yours dishes backs, thankyou'! *Associated British Ports*

Left South Wales Echo, 7 July 1941. South Wales Echo/Media Wales Ltd

Right South Wales Echo, 27 March 1941. South Wales Echo/Media Wales Ltd

SEAMEN'S WELFARE

Facilities at South Wales Ports

In accordance with the development of its plans for the welfare of seamen using British ports, the Ministry of Labour and National Service has now appointed seamen's welfare officers at eight of the most important ports in the country.

Among these are the ports of Cardiff and Barry for which an office has been opened at No. 2 Bute-crescent, Cardiff, where the Seamen's Welfare Officer has taken up his duties. A Port Welfare Committee, representative of all the interests involved, is to be established by the Ministry and will have as its terms of reference the co-ordination and further development of welfare work amongst seamen in the port on the lines approved by the International Labour Office of the League of Nations.

This committee, whose secretary will be the Seamen's Welfare Officer, will also have a special responsibility for the development of co-operation between British and Allied and neutral associations and in helping the latter to secure welfare facilities of all kinds for Allied and foreign seamen using the port.

It is anticipated that the preliminary work already accomplished by the Allied and Neutral Hospitality Committee, which was set up in Cardiff at the end of last year under the chairmanship of Commander T. J. Linberry, R.N., will prove of great value to the main Port Welfare Committee in its prosecution of the Government's wider plans.

FORMER CARDIFF PLEASURE BOAT SHOT DOWN RAIDER

IT was disclosed last night that the peace-time pleasure steamer, Lorna Doone, built as long ago as 1891, has destroyed one Dornier and possibly two.

The vessel, known to thousands of holiday-makers who in peace-time crossed between Southampton and the Isle of Wight, now has the designation of "H.M. Paddle Minesweeper."

Before being sent to the South of England, the Lorna Doone was a popular holiday steamer in the Bristol Channel Service.

At that time the Lorna Doone was the fastest ship on the Bristol Channel passenger service.

When she was bombed and machine-gunned by three Dornier 215's on Wednesday she attacked them with all her guns. One plane was seen to be on fire and losing height rapidly.

The Admiralty stated last night that this machine was considered to have been destroyed. A second was badly hit, and a coastguard station reported that large pieces were seen falling off it. The third machine made off in the haze.

Dodged Bombs

Two wounded were the only casualties in the Lorna Doone. The vessel received only superficial damage to the bridge and deckhouses from machine-gun bullets. Four large bombs were dropped, but she avoided them by skilful manoeuvring.

The Lorna Doone, which is commanded by Temporary Lieutenant T. W. Sherrin, R.N.V.R., is of only 410 tons gross. Her former owners were the South of England Royal Mail Steam Packet Co., Ltd.

Above and right Heroism of the Cardiff crew aboard a former pleasure steamer: extracts from the *South Wales Echo* of 4 April and 3 May 1941. *South Wales Echo/Media Wales Ltd*

Lorna Doone Gunner Was Cardiff Boy

He Fought Off Dorniers' Attack

HERO of a paddle minesweeper which brought down two out of three attacking enemy aircraft is Able-seaman G. Bee, a Cardiff boy, of 61, Woodville-road, Cathays, whose father, Mr. F. H. Bee, of 71, Crwys-road, Cardiff, is manager of a shop at Bridgend.

Able-seaman Bee was the gunner on board the paddle-minesweeper Lorna Doone, the fifty - year - old pleasure boat which used to ply between Southampton and the Isle of Wight, and is now engaged on the sterner duties of war.

Able-seaman Bee

This gallant little vessel, known to many thousands of holidaymakers, was attacked by three Dornier 215's who carried out machine-gun and bombing attacks from low clouds. Four large bombs were dropped, but the Lorna Doone engaged the enemy with her guns.

Two Hit

One of the raiders was seen to be on fire and losing height rapidly; the second was also seen to be badly hit, and shortly afterwards a coastguard reported that large pieces were seen to be falling from it. The third made good its escape in poor visibility.

The only casualties on the minesweeper were two wounded, and the ship suffered only superficial damage.

Able-seaman Bee was at his Lewis gun throughout the action, and according to accounts of the engagement was responsible for the downfall of the German raiders.

Twenty-one years of age, he attended Cathays School, and was employed by Messrs. Preston and Thomas before joining the Navy at age of 16. Before the war he served in the Mediterranean, and was on the Repulse when it took the King and Queen to Canada for their American tour.

DEEPER LOADING

War Time Shipping Measure

The Chamber of Shipping is considering proposals just issued by the Ministry of Shipping designed to increase the cargo space of certain vessels.

These proposals include a reduction of the freeboard or "open" shelter deck vessels subject to certain safeguards, among them the closing of the shelter deck to allow this additional cargo to be carried.

It is understood that the proposals are being put forward as a war-time measure and in an effort to make the greatest possible use in the national interest of all serviceable tonnage.

Above South Wales Echo, 2 May 1941. South Wales Echo/Media Wales Ltd

Right This map, issued to the Luftwaffe on 30 November 1941, was actually a 1920 Ordnance Survey map overprinted with bombing targets and symbols representing the type of bomb suitable for them: incendiary, high-explosive, delayed-action and the silent but deadly parachute mines. *Pontypridd Library*

Opposite below German Luftwaffe photographs Nos 85 and 102 from the pack GB7, BB32, given to aircraft navigators with the overprinted maps. The pack contained photographs of targets in South Wales. The text with the picture on the left reads: 'Queen Alexandra Dock, and the docks of Cardiff (Glam) on right, Queen Alexandra Dock, with tank stores and pumping house chimney, at bottom right, Cold Store and Bonded Warehouses, directly behind is the Timber Storage area. At the top right of this dock is Roath Dock and Roath Basin, which connects Roath Dock to Bute East Dock. Next to East Dock, on the left, is Bute West Dock.'

The other photo has the following information: 'Docks steelworks in Cardiff, photographed at 1000 feet high. The steelworks of Guest Keen and Baldwin's, Iron and Steel Co Ltd (Dowlais Works), east of Bute Dock. Situated on 47 hectares is the Coke Works extension, producing 9,000 tons of raw heat to make 7,000 tons of coke, 10,000 tons of raw steel, converted by flattening and rolling into armour plate for aircraft.' In 1939 the steelworks employed 600 men.

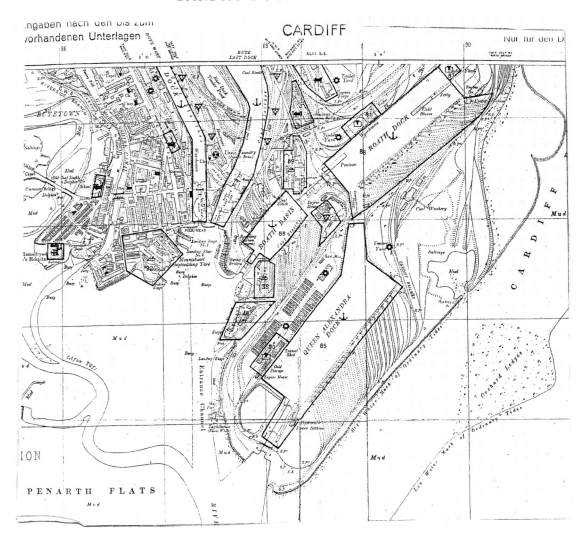

The RAF's fighters were superior to the Luftwaffe's, but early in the Battle of Britain it was realised that many Allied pilots had no armoured protection behind their cockpit seat. This was rectified by the insertion of a sheet of armoured plate, and the Dowlais Works was one of many that made this plating. Because of it, many more fighter pilots high in the sky during those summer months lived to fight again. *Pontypridd Library*

Immediate Declaration Of War On Japan
—MR. CHURCHILL

Mr. Churchill announced to-day that the British Cabinet, which met at 12 o'clock this morning, had been authorised to make an immediate declaration of war on Japan.

"As soon as I heard last night that Japan had attacked the United States, I felt it necessary that Parliament should be immediately summoned," said the Premier.

"I spoke to President Roosevelt last night with a view to arranging the time of our respective declarations," added the Premier.

Instructions were sent to our Ambassador at Tokio, and communication was despatched to the Japanese Chargé d'Affaires at one o'clock to-day stating that in view of Japan's wanton acts of unprovoked aggression the British Government informed them that a state of war existed between the two countries.

The Japanese began a landing in British territory in Northern Malaya at about 6—(1 a.m. local time)—yesterday and they were immediately engaged by our forces which were ready. (Cheers.)

Netherlands Follows

Home Office measures against Japanese nationals were set in motion at 10.45 last night. The House will see therefore that no time has been lost, and we are actually ahead of our engagements.

The Royal Netherlands Government at once marked their solidarity with Great Britain, and the United States at 3 a.m. by stating that as a consequence of Japan's action a state of war now exists between the kingdom of the Netherlands and Japan.

Mr. Churchill said he had sent a message yesterday to the ruler of Thailand telling him that we would regard an invasion of his country as an attack on ourselves. He had also sent a message to General Chiang Kai-Shek assuring him that thenceforward we would face the common foe together.

Jap Treachery

Japanese Envoys were ordered to prolong their mission in the U.S.A. in order to keep conversations going while a surprise attack was being prepared and before a declaration of war could be delivered.

"No one can doubt," he said, "that every effort to bring about a peaceful solution has been made by the Government of the United States and that immense patience has been shown in the face of grow-

Left From the *South Wales Echo*, 8 December 1941. *South Wales Echo/Media Wales Ltd*

Below Another map issued by the Luftwaffe on 30 November 1941, based on the 1920 Ordnance Survey map. Note the marking of strategically important railway bridges. *Pontypridd Library*

1942

Above Streamlined LMS 'Princess Coronation' Class locomotive No 6220 *Coronation* is being discharged from the deck of the SS *Pacific Pioneer* on its return from America on 16 February 1942. Actually, the real identity of this 4-6-2 locomotive was No 6229 *Duchess of Hamilton*, which had been renamed and renumbered for a tour of the United States as part of the New York World's Fair in

January 1939. (The engine was de-streamlined in 1948.) *Associated British Ports*

Below These cases are awaiting shipment to the colonies, circa 1942. In one of the doorways of No 1 Shed stand two dockers and a member of HM Forces; all three look a little apprehensive, perhaps because of the photograph being taken. The cases are bound for Hamilton, Bermuda, and Kingston, Jamaica. *Associated British Ports*

Below In May 1942 these Stothert & Pitt cranes are hard at work discharging bags of sugar from the SS *Baron Ramsey* into No 1 Shed at Queen Alexandra Dock, using battery-operated Hyster Ransome electric trucks, which were used extensively for shed work in the docks. On No 2 road a shipment of timber is being loaded onto bogie bolster wagons, while on the Stage Road some open wagons that have seen better days wait alongside the loading bay. *Associated British Ports*

Bottom This is the GWR Fire Brigade at Cardiff Docks, photographed on 17 June 1942 outside the Pierhead

Building main entrance; they were a voluntary body, made up from the docks' permanent staff. On either side are their trailer pumps, which were manufactured by either Dennis, Godiva or Coventry Climax, and could pump several hundred gallons of water per minute, either from street hydrants or, in this case, a dock. A close look at the photo reveals the outline of a centrifugal pump with its input connector (4-inch diameter), while the suction hose and basket strainer are situated down each side of the pump; the fireman at the left-hand end of the second row has his right hand on the suction hose. During the war these pumps were usually towed by an Austin K2 Auxiliary Towing Vehicle.

The fireman third from the right in the front row is wearing a standard double-breasted cavalry twill fire tunic, which was in use right up until the late 1960s. This provided an overlap in the front, and was of a better quality material than the uniforms worn by rest of the firemen pictured here; their tunics were mass-produced and gave very little protection from heat or water. Each fireman was issued with a wooden-handled fireman's axe, a belt and pouch made of canvas with usually a chrome buckle, a steel black-painted helmet, and a gasmask bag. The officer in the centre, with the chrome rank markings, is possibly a Company Commander, while the men standing at the back on the right, wearing medals, are First World War veterans. *Associated British Ports*

Right The 100-ton floating crane *Simson III* is discharging the fore (or stem) section of Tank Landing Craft No 427 at Roath Dock in November 1942. This LCT Mark 3 was designed to be broken down for transportation. *Associated British Ports*

Right Assisted by two tugs, Simson III is now carrying the deck section LCT No 427. *Associated British Ports*

Below The assembled Tank Landing Craft at Roath Dock's Grain Jetty, behind which is an armed Merchant Navy vessel. In the background are the Lewis Hunter luffing cranes at Dowlais Wharf, and behind them is the GKN steelworks. *Associated British Ports*

Left On Friday 27 November 1942 a cargo of USA 'S160' Class engines and tenders has arrived aboard the SS *Pacific Enterprise*. Their wheels are sitting on baulks of wood, with wooden blocks between the wheels to prevent movement and damage; the deck cargo is also secured with steel hawsers. On the right, pitched at an angle, is one of the ship's wartime quick-release life-rafts. *Associated British Ports*

Left One of the American-manufactured 'S160s' is lifted by the floating crane as a party of onlookers anxiously watches the progress. This front view provides a good view of the Westinghouse brake pump attached to the smokebox door. *Associated British Ports*

Below This side view of 2-8-0 No 1609 shows its Walschaerts valve gear and connecting rods, all cast in bright steel. Above the two central wheels is one of the two Westinghouse brake main air reservoirs. The wooden shuttering around the side windows and the back of the cab has been removed, and we can also see the balanced lifting beam suspended above the locomotive's boiler. *Associated British Ports*

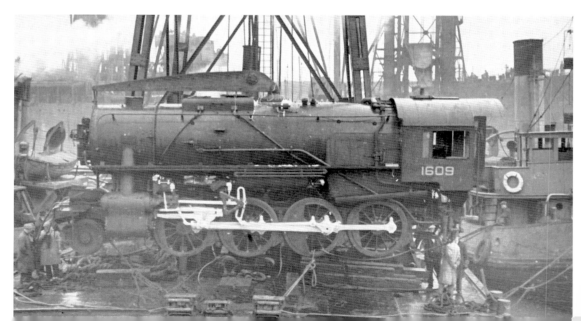

Right   Simson III lifts one of the '∫160s' from ship to barge for ferrying to the dockside. This 100-ton GWR floating crane was a real help with cargoes of this size and weight – it was a real workhorse! *Associated British Ports*

Below   No 1609 is draped in the American 'Stars and Stripes' and the British 'Union Jack', the national flags providing a symbol of common unity in a just cause, the fight against oppression. *Associated British Ports*

1943

With the lack of manpower caused by so many men from all walks of life being in the forces, women are now filling jobs traditionally held by men. Inside A Shed, Queen Alexandra Dock, circa 1943, the women are moving barrels, boxes and tyres – nothing too large to be handled by them and their sack trolleys. *Associated British Ports*

Inside the sheds a woman porter is driving a motorised goods trolley, probably one of the battery-operated Hyster Ransomes. While this photograph was probably taken for propaganda purposes as well as to boost public moral, in the background men and women porters get on with their daily work. *Associated British Ports*

These women porters are unloading a railway wagon – three boxes on a sack truck, or four if you were on piecework, but your knuckles got rubbed and sore from the friction of that extra box! These wire-banded cardboard boxes are perhaps not too heavy, especially as they are being transported in a 5ton 11cwt tare railway wagon; however, these women porters had to be strong to handle the varied cargoes entering, being stored in and leaving these warehouses. *Associated British Ports*

Above By 5 February 1943 repairs have been effected following the air raid of 3/4 March 1941 (see pages 108-11), when high-explosive bombs damaged the permanent way, telephone communications, and the Wagon Repairs premises on the north side of Bute East Dock Branch No 2. In the background is the silhouette of the GKN steelworks. Because of their extensive rail network, these docks were always going to be vulnerable to bombing. *Associated British Ports*

Below Repairs have also been made to the sidings hit during the same air raid on the north side of Bute East Dock. An interesting feature is the swan-neck lamp, with its ladder and back rest, so different from the bracketed lamps that can also be seen. *Associated British Ports*

£1,450 FOR SPITFIRE

Lord Beaverbrook has expressed his "immense pleasure" at receiving from the "Powell Duffryn Staff Spitfire Fund" a cheque for £1,450 towards the purchase of a Spitfire.

The amount has been collected from members of the staff, helped by certain of the directors of the following companies or associated companies of the Powell Duffryn group: Powell Duffryn Associated Collieries, Ltd.; Gueret, Llewellyn, and Merrett, Ltd.; Stephenson Clark and Associated Companies, Ltd.; Maris Export and Trading Company, Ltd.; Pyman Watson and Co., Ltd.; Cambrian Wagon Works, Ltd.; Coal Distributors (South Wales), Ltd.

The amount collected from the staff is, of course, in addition to the contributions they have made to the various local Spitfire funds in the United Kingdom.

Above A report in the *South Wales Echo* of 17 February 1941 regarding money raised towards a Spitfire by employees of the Powell Duffryn group. *South Wales Echo/Media Wales Ltd*

Above right and below left RAF Hawker Sea Hurricane Z4924 is being hoisted aboard the CAM ship (Catapult Aircraft Merchantman) SS *Empire Gale* on 9 April 1943. Once aboard, the aircraft is placed on the ship's 'Hurricat' catapult launcher. Z4924 was operated by the Merchant Ship Fighter Unit based at RAF Speke, and once launched would provide convoy protection against German bombers or operate against German reconnaissance aircraft. On his return to the ship, the pilot would ditch in the sea as close as possible, whereupon aircraft and pilot would be hoisted aboard by the ship's derrick (not so clever an idea when operating on one of the frequent convoys to the Russian ports, where the waters were freezing and treacherous). Usually these CAM ships were used with Mediterranean or Baltic convoys, and the combination of ship and plane was invaluable, although at a high cost in terms of pilots and aircraft. Long-range fuel tanks beneath the wings were

introduced in August 1941, and these increased the aircraft's flying range, and the catapults became more powerful to cope with the increase in the aircraft's weight.

I am grateful to Stuart Hadaway, Assistant Curator of the RAF Museum, London, for providing the 'Movement Card' history of Z4924. It was delivered new to No 10 Maintenance Unit, RAF Hullavington, on 3 June 1941. It served on the CAM ship from 9 April 1943 until it was 'struck off charge' on 2 November 1944. This appears to have been due to 'natural causes' rather than a combat loss, as by then Hurricanes were being phased out. It is hard to say if Z4924 saw action; usually Sea Hurricanes that were launched had to be ditched into the sea and were lost, although some did make it back to friendly territory. Between April 1943 and 1944 it may have been used for training or kept in a depot; the frequent damage recorded on the card may have been as a result of training accidents, or damage inflicted by, for example, inclement weather on board ship. *Associated British Ports*

Below right *South Wales Echo*, 18 May 1943. *South Wales Echo/Media Wales Ltd*

SHOW YOUR APPRECIATION OF THEIR SACRIFICE DURING

WINGS for VICTORY WEEK

MAY 15th to MAY 22nd

AN APPEAL BY

E. ROBERTS
LIMITED

KINGSWAY HOUSE,
PARK HALL BUILDINGS and 15 and 16, MOUNT STUART SQ.,
CARDIFF.

Right In 1940 the King's Wharf Cold Store was built under Ministry of Food instructions, and was one of the most modern in the country. It was a steel-framed brick structure of five floors, containing 26 chambers in six sections of approximately equal size. It was equipped with nine 2-ton electric lifts, and the total refrigerated space provided was 1,018,612 cubic feet, which was capable of accommodating about 10,000 tons of goods. The Cold Store was built alongside the deep-water berth of King's Wharf) and was served by both rail and road for the speedy receiving and distribution of refrigerated cargoes. In addition to meat, it handled butter, cheese, eggs, fish and other foodstuffs requiring cold storage accommodation, and was also a distribution centre.

In about 1943 frozen New Zealand lamb is being weighed before being put into storage in the Cold Store, which was used to its full storage capacity. These scales would be kept accurate by regular checks by Ministry of Food officials. *Associated British Ports*

Right A woman porter is about to push loaded trolleys into one of the Cold Store lifts – not an easy task as each trolley carried approximately 330lb of frozen meat. *Associated British Ports*

Left Having bridged the gap between the flatbed wagon on the Staging Road (next to the loading bay) and the GWR 'Conflat' (a 'Lowflat' with a GWR insulated meat container attached), the porter gingerly steadies the boxes of imported 'Dawnkist' frozen Canadian salmon before releasing the rope on this bale sling at King's Wharf. Before the war, in 1932, the *GWR Magazine* reported that, in order to meet the requirements of the meat trade, the company's directors had authorised the provision of 125 insulated and 75 ventilated containers for the conveyance of chilled and fresh meat respectively. *Associated British Ports*

Top This early design of hospital ship, the *Atlantis*, is about to leave Queen Alexandra Dock, circa 1943. She was painted white all over with a broad green stripe and red crosses to tell the enemy that she was under the protection of the Geneva Convention. During the night she would be lit up, with searchlights permanently directed at the red crosses. Sadly these ships did not always escape being sunk. During both World Wars enemy submarines struck at them with torpedoes in the belief that they were carrying ammunition or war supplies; true or not, it was a clear case of 'loose talk sinks ships'.

Above the ship can be seen a barrage balloon. These were part of the scenery during those dark times, and caused great hindrance to the Luftwaffe. The steel cables that secured them could quite easily cut through the wing of an enemy plane, so to avoid them the German pilots had to climb higher or make an unorthodox bombing run, putting the bomb-aimer/navigator off his pre-planned attack. RAF airmen and female WAAFs of No 953 (BB) Squadron RAF, supplied by No 14 Barrage Balloon Centre, maintained the balloons, repaired any leaks and moved them around with a jeep or lorry, helping to uphold the safety of Cardiff. *Associated British Ports*

Middle This is the SS *Larges Bay*, with anti-aircraft guns on the foredeck and quick-release life-rafts in position, circa 1943. Her stem is of a vertical design, and both masts (fore and main) carry wide crosstrees. Of a type designed in wartime, this co-opted cargo vessel is certainly due a spell in dry dock, but ships, like people, had to make do. Another barrage balloon can be seen in the distance. *Associated British Ports*

Bottom This photograph, taken from the roof of the Cold Store, shows the movable coal hoists on the south side of Queen Alexandra Dock, which could be moved to suit the configuration of the ship's hold, and more than one hoist could be used to speed up a vessel's turn-round. As this photograph shows, two vessels are under their respective coaling chutes getting ready to be bunkered up (for the boilers) or to take on coal (for cargo). *Associated British Ports*

The air raid of 18 May 1943 started in the northern area of Cardiff, with the Luftwaffe bombers following the Cardiff Railway line in an easterly direction and releasing their deadly cargo as they passed over the houses of Whitchurch, Rhiwbina, Birchgrove and Heath, before heading south for the centre of Cardiff and the GWR's General station. They then headed towards Bute Street and Cardiff Docks, and more high-explosive bombs and parachute mines were dropped in the docks area. Bute Street railway station was hit, together with Guest, Keen & Baldwin's steelworks, the Crown Fuel Works, the John Williams steelworks and the Cardiff Boat Building Company's premises. For the East Dock area and many other places it was 83 minutes of death and destruction. The following nine photographs of the damage caused are from the Associated British Ports archive.

South Wales Echo, 18 May 1943. *South Wales Echo/Media Wales Ltd*

Important Supply Port Of Cardiff Attacked, Say Germans

Considerable Damage & a Number of Casualties

Others Feared Buried Beneath Wreckage

In a raid lasting over an hour on what the Germans describe as the "important supply harbour of Cardiff last night—it was one of the sharpest experienced since 1941—extensive damage was caused to dwelling-houses, shops and stores, and up to this morning a number of bodies had been recovered and a good many people have been taken to hospital.

It is feared that at least 20 others are still buried beneath the wreckage of their homes.

Among the dead are three Waafs. They were killed outright when a small high explosive bomb made a direct hit on a shelter. Four others were injured.

The Air Ministry and Ministry of Home Security communique states: "Enemy bombers were over South-west England and South Wales last night and dropped bombs at several places.

"In one district in South Wales damage was done and there were a number of casualties, some of them fatal.

"Elsewhere a little damage was done but no one was seriously injured.

HEAVIER TYPE OF BOMBERS

"A few fighter-bombers were over South-east England and the Greater London area during the night. Bombs were dropped, causing slight damage and a small number of casualties. Three enemy aircraft were destroyed."

Except for the fact that the raids were more widely extended they were very similar to the previous night's attacks. For the most part the raiders were of the fighter-bomber type, although in the raids on South Wales and the South-west

In the glare of an early morning moonlight heightened by flares a sharp air attack struck the Welsh town.

The night will long be remembered for the heroic rescue work and the fortitude and presence of mind of those unfortunate people who were buried under their wrecked homes.

A *South Wales Echo* reporter spent most of the night in a modern avenue of one of the town's residential suburbs.

He writes: When I arrived shortly after the explosion the scene was one of sheer destruction. Eight houses had been completely flattened and all round roofs of adjoining property had been ripped off, doors from their sockets and windows broken everywhere. It seemed that not a single house within a certain radius escaped.

Trapped Policeman

Wardens were already active checking up the residents. It was known that a few families were buried, and for hours rescue parties tunnelled a way through the mass of debris. It seemed that no-one could survive, but the rescuers were rewarded when they heard the voice of a man, first faintly but gradually getting stronger and stronger. It was known that a well-known member of the police force lived in this house, and that his little daughter was with him.

"It's my chest," he was heard to say. Then came the brave voice of the little girl.

Thus encouraged, the rescue parties worked almost in a frenzy to reach the trapped father and child. The voices became louder, and at last the leading member of the rescue squad could reach the father with outstretched hand. But there was still another agonising hour before both were finally brought out. It was a miracle that they were alive.

Killed in "Morrison"

Just alongside another rescue party was working equally hard to reach a family of three who had taken refuge in a Morrison indoor shelter. Here, again, after moving a mass of masonry and hacking a tunnel from the back of the house, the rescuers were able to reach the imprisoned family. Two were dead and one alive.

Among the dead in this area was Mr. Ifor Williams and his wife. Mr. Williams was the assistant secretary of the Cardiff Cymro-dorian Society. The daughter escaped.

RAID ON SOUTH WALES COAST TOWN

FROM PAGE ONE

The attack was widespread, but the few fires that were caused were quickly brought under control.

Amongst the fatal casualties were three members of the Women's Auxiliary Air Force. They fell in the front line doing their duty.

Put Family Safe, Killed

A number of high explosive and incendiary bombs fell in a working class district. In one street three houses were demolished as a

School Gutted

In yet another street two houses were destroyed by high explosives and the street was evacuated.

A very large number of incendiary bombs caused some fires in houses in the same area. Most, however, were got out without doing much damage but an elementary school was gutted.

Two high explosive bombs fell in back gardens between two other streets in the same area and made huge craters. Earth and debris was flung over a very wide area and shelters were damaged, but luckily no one was injured.

A housing estate had a few direct hits and here, too, the various services toiled through the night. Indeed, there was such a demand on A.R.P. personnel that reinforcements were rushed from neighbouring authorities and rendered valiant aid.

Houses Collapsed

At one wrecked site where four houses had collapsed like a pack of cards they worked until they had barely a gasp left in a vain but valiant effort to reach an aged couple.

In a night of many escapes perhaps one of the most amazing was that of the young wife of an R.A.F. man. With her little girl, she was in a house which was completely wrecked, but when a warden and a member of the Home Guard reached the house within a few minutes of the explosion they were able to extricate both mother and daughter from the pile of rubble unscratched.

It seems that immediately following the crash they began to crawl their way through the wreckage and had reached a gap in the wall when help came. As always, one of the features of the night's ordeal was the neighbourliness and companionship shown by all. Although the local authority put into immediate use their rest centre scheme, families whose homes were gone were quickly accommodated by neighbours.

Still Buried

In another district a high explosive bomb fell in the roadway between two air raid shelters which were crowded with people. No one in either of the shelters was injured, but adjacent premises were wrecked. In one of these premises, a hotel, the licensee, an elderly woman, and her son-in-law and daughter were in a Morrison shelter. The hotel was demolished, but the occupants of the shelter, although buried beneath heavy debris, were rescued unharmed.

In the house next door to the hotel two women were killed, and to-day rescuers continued their search for another woman and a man who are believed to have been in the house when the bomb was dropped. Neither has been traced, and it is assumed that they are still buried under the wreckage.

In a South Wales country district two people were killed and four injured when raiders dropped a few high explosives, also flares and incendiaries.

A seaside town had showers of high explosives and incendiaries and at one house three A.T.S. girls were slightly injured. There were several direct hits on property without a fatality or serious injury, and in one locality Mrs. Ann Richards, aged 70, was rescued together with her son before their home and the house next door was completely gutted.

Above High-explosive bombs caused damage to the permanent way and the Crown Fuel Works during the air raid of the early morning of 18 May 1943. During the raid three German aircraft were shot down.

Left The offices of John Williams Steel Ltd on East Moors Road were also hit.

Left Bomb damage to the Boat Building Company premises at Queen Alexandra Dock.

This badly damaged vessel in East Dock is believed to be the SS *Emebank*.

Debris in the cargo hold of the SS *Emebank*. The contents of the crates were parts of a military tender, stencilled 'Canmec' and 'Canmilitary'.

This damaged vessel is alongside the pontoon of the Channel Pontoon Company, in the harbour adjacent to the Channel Dry Dock entrance.

Top Bombs also hit buildings and the running roads leading to and from the movable coaling hoists on the south side of Queen Alexandra Dock.

Middle The barge used by the docks' divers is seen at Junction Lock. In peacetime the divers would use the barge to make regular inspections of the dock walls, and it would be moved as required to provide a working platform. However, on 18 May 1943, the morning after one of the biggest air raids on Cardiff, the divers are looking for any signs of bomb damage to the walls or bed of the lock, or for any unexploded bombs lying at the bottom. No task carried out in these dark silted waters was easy, but this was a dangerous one.

Bottom During the raid high-explosive bombs were dropped on the area covered by these Marshalling Sidings, damaging buildings, lineside huts, rolling stock and the permanent way. Later in the day the clean-up and repair gangs got busy.

Top On 1 March 1944 in Queen Alexandra Dock we have a 'beam-on' view of hospital ship No 41 *Amra* taking on stores and provisions from the Cold Store at King's Wharf. *Associated British Ports*

Middle The captured German vessel *Tafelberg* is moored on the south side of Queen Alexandra Dock alongside the coaling hoists. Her forward gun can be seen, behind which is a mast protruding from a set of twin kingposts. Framed by this is the wheelhouse, on top of the navigation bridge; having the bridge so far forward allows room on deck for large unwieldy cargoes. At the mid-section is another similar mast and kingpost arrangement, this set having the Finnish style of ventilators attached. Towards the stern is the last set of kingposts, which frame what appear to be twin side funnels. A seaman can be glimpsed standing on the bracing of the stern kingposts, with his arm outstretched, while standing on the bracing of the mid-section kingposts is another tiny figure, stooping over. The ship was subsequently renamed *Empire Heritage* and became a welcome addition to the Allied fleet. *Associated British Ports*

Bottom The SS *Deseado*, served by a battery of six Stothert & Pitt electric cranes, is discharging her cargo as quickly as possible into the Cold Store at King's Wharf in March 1944. *Associated British Ports*

Top Meanwhile, away from the battle-scarred ships and the shouting of men, we enter the calmness of the cattle lairs on the north side of Roath Inner Lock (near the Commercial Dry Dock), where horses are tethered inside the dockside compound, circa 1944. A group of seamen on the vessel in the background, in Roath Inner Lock, make use of a moment on the weather deck to view this peaceful scene before proceeding through the lock into Roath Dock. On top of the wheelhouse is the box-design framework of a radio receiver/transmitter. Two different types of ship's boat can be seen: the lifeboat on the right carries the number 4, while the boat on the left is a whaler. *Associated British Ports*

Middle This Royal visit of Their Majesties Queen Elizabeth and King George VI, with the future Queen, Princess Elizabeth, in attendance, took place on 30 March 1944. The Royal group are being greeted by dock officials at the steps of the main entrance into the Pierhead Building. This visit may have been linked to a morale-boosting tour of the City of Cardiff, to meet the people and inspect the war damage. From left to right are Colonel Sir Gerald Bruce (Senior Regional Commissioner Civil Defence and Lord Lieutenant of Glamorgan), HM Queen Elizabeth, HRH Princess Elizabeth, HM King George VI, Hugh Roberts (Port Regional Director of all South Wales GWR Docks), N. J. Thomas (Chief GWR Docks Manager, South Wales Docks, shaking hands), L. E. Ford (Assistant Chief GWR Docks Manager, South Wales Docks) and D. G. Hoppins (GWR Dock Manager of Cardiff Docks). *Associated British Ports*

Bottom In November 1944 another event is taking place outside the front entrance of the Pierhead Building. This time it's the presentation of a Royal Humane Society parchment to Leading Fireman Morgan. From left to right are Mr David Roberts (Mechanical Engineers Dept), another unknown member of that department, the General Cargo and Docks Manager, an unknown uniformed person (a Forces Liaison Officer wearing the First World War battledress of a mounted regiment, the RHS representative, a uniformed

Captain (Dock Master), Leading Fireman Morgan, and an unknown Station Officer with three red embroidered bars on his shoulder epaulettes (having control over a single fire station and three watches, Red, White and Blue). Leading Fireman Morgan's rank is designated by the single red stripe on his helmet, and a single red embroidered bar on his shoulder epaulettes. *Associated British Ports*

Top The south-east corner of Roath Dock was known as the 'Prairie', and when photographed in March 1944, only a matter of months before D Day, it was just one of many transit camps scattered around the South West of England and South Wales. Stores and supplies are building up – tents, crates, mobile generators, transporters, cranes and vehicles of all types, including at least one fuel truck. In the foreground is a mixture of open wagons of the 'Big Four' as well as one private owner wagon belonging to the City of Birmingham Gas Department; some of the wagons carry sawn planks, others pit props, while some are tarpaulin-sheeted, perhaps for security purposes or just for protection against the elements. *Associated British Ports*

Middle Camouflaged warship No 72 visits Cardiff Docks, circa 1944. It was during the First World War, when the German submarine campaign was at its worst, that Admiralty instructions were issued in late 1916 that dazzle paint should be applied to ships in dry dock, and as many as two or three dozen vessels were to be painted each week. There is no doubt that the men who worked in the dry docks,

in both World Wars, did a superb job. Sadly, many of the ships that arrived in Cardiff and other ports carried dead and wounded servicemen, it was in those dry docks that they were removed, a job carried out professionally by the dockers themselves. *Associated British Ports*

Bottom In Queen Alexandra Dock, seen from the lock entrance circa 1944, are four moored 'Liberty' ships, all armed. For many years the area on the left was designated for used as two graving docks; however, this never happened, and today this waterfront is the timber berth for Messrs F. W. Morgan Ltd. *Associated British Ports*

Above Diesel-electric locomotives are being unloaded from the 'sea train' *Texas* to the quayside of Queen Alexandra Dock by the MOWT 10 60-ton self-propelled floating crane on 10 March 1944. These 'sea train' vessels had three decks of railway tracks, more than enough to ensure a good and safe cargo of locomotives. The crane is actually floating between the quayside and the ship. Note its canvas-covered bridge (known as a 'Dodger'). These Whitcomb diesels have been manufactured in the USA and are a part of a shipment that, once unloaded, will be moved to the USA Transportation Corps depot at Ebbw Junction engine repair shop, near Newport, before going over the English Channel en route to France later in the year. *Associated British Ports*

Below The American-built diesels are now on the Roath Storage Sidings, coupled up and waiting to be taken to the USA Transportation Corps depot at Newport. This scene was photographed on 3 June 1944 (D Day minus 3), and soon the invasion will be a reality. After D Day the locos will end up working in France. Behind the diesels, on the embankment, can be seen private owner wagons of the Alloa Coal Co Ltd, from Rother Vale and Colliness Collieries, behind which is a rake of iron-ore hoppers, all carrying the initials MOT. *Associated British Ports*

There is plenty of cargo aboard the *Texas* on 10 March 1944, so much so that the 60-ton self-propelled floating crane now has the assistance of the 100-ton floating crane *Simson III*, the jib of which can be seen beyond the vessel. Being unloaded is an American M26 tank transporter tractor with an armoured cab, built by the Pacific Car & Foundry Co. These transporters were mostly used by the United States Army. *Associated British Ports*

During the same month, this very busy scene shows the SS *Deseado* discharging meat and dairy products into the Cold Store at King's Wharf and into the railway vans on the Stage Road. In the background, just past the Communication Passage, are the Crown Fuel Works buildings. *Associated British Ports*

The SS *Mobile City* is at berth alongside the Lewis Hunter luffing cranes at the General Cargo Quay, Roath Dock, circa 1944, while the cranes discharge part of her cargo. On the water side of the vessel the 100-ton floating crane *Simson III*, assisted into position by a tug, receives the ship's cargo of crated vehicles. Under the legs of the luffing cranes on the Water Road is a rake of GWR vans. *Associated British Ports*

Meat is being discharged from the SS *Port Jackson* into the King's Wharf Cold Store and the waiting railway vans on the Staging Road on 21 March 1944. It's a busy time for the Stothert & Pitt crane drivers and the Cold Store porters alike. The photo provides a good view of the ventilators at the top of the kingposts (also known as Sampson posts) on this typical prefabricated American ship. *Associated British Ports*

On the same day the cargo hold of the *Port Jackson* is framed by the jibs of the electric cranes in this interesting view. The net is full of meat destined for the Cold Store. Because the crane driver would be unsighted during this operation, the two men standing at the side of the hatch would act as signallers. The four motorised winches, one for each corner of the hatch, operate the ship's derricks, which have been swung over the ship's side, clear of the quayside crane movements. Note the clutter around the deck area, made up of hatch beams and covers together with other debris such as loose timbers from the hold, used to prevent movement of the cargo while at sea. *Associated British Ports*

The 50-ton improvised floating crane is in use carrying a military tracked vehicle across Queen Alexandra Dock with the help of two tug boats, circa 1944. The crane's base was constructed by placing the hulls of two barges together. Its derrick-style crane, with its 100-ton companion *Simson III*, did conspicuous work in the docks during the war years. *Associated British Ports*

FRANCE INVADED ON 70-MILE FRONT

"D" Day **"D" Day**

4,000 Ships, 11,000 First-Line Planes Take Part
—Says Churchill

Beachheads Established : Allies "Slashing Inland" : Pilots' Pictures

SUPPORTED by planes in tremendous numbers and a mighty combined Anglo-U.S. naval force, the long-awaited invasion started at 6 a.m. to-day and reports coming to hand almost every minute from the battle areas indicate that progress is so far satisfactory.

The landings have taken place over a 70-mile stretch of the Normandy coast, extending from Dieppe to the Cherbourg peninsular.

TANKS GO ASHORE

A statement issued this afternoon by the Eighth U.S.A.A.F. Photo Reconnaissance base says that photo reconnaissance pilots back from the landings report that the Allies have established beachheads and are "slashing inland."

The German News Agency says tanks have landed in the area of Arromanches, a small town on the coast midway between Havre and Cherbourg, about 20 miles north-west of Caen.

Paris radio this afternoon said the Germans are putting up very stiff resistance in the Caen area. The town area itself has been sorely tried. The enemy appears to be penetrating deeper inland.

In the House of Commons Mr. Churchill revealed that an immense armada of 4,000 ships with several

thousand smaller craft took part in the invasion.

Massed airborne landings, he said, have been successfully effected behind the enemy lines, landings on beaches at various places were proceeding, and the fire of the shore batteries has been largely quelled.

The Premier also disclosed that 11,000 first-line aircraft are engaged in supporting operations.

A Reuter correspondent telegraphs this afternoon that transport planes, after unloading, are returning with few losses.

Gen. Eisenhower, Supreme Commander of the Allied armies, made the first official announcement in a communiqué issued shortly before 10 o'clock and described as "Communiqué No. 1."

In a single laconic phrase it said:

"Allied naval forces supported by strong air forces began landing Allied armies this morning on the northern coast of France."

Soon afterwards it was announced that H.M. the King will broadcast to the nation at nine o'clock this evening.

HITLER TAKES COMMAND

Gen. Montgomery is in charge of the Army group carrying out the assault, with British, Canadian and U.S. forces under his command.

According to a report received in London, Hitler is taking personal command of all anti-invasion operations. He is said to be surrounded by a staff including four marshals and is believed to have moved his headquarters to "a place somewhere" in Northern France.

Hitler's marshals are said to be Rundstedt, titular Commander - in - Chief; Rommel, Inspector-General; Sperie, in charge of air forces, and Blaskowitz, deputy to Rommel.

Gen. Eisenhower broadcast to the people of Western Europe at the outset of the invasion.

"A landing was made this morning," he said, "on the coast of France by troops of the Allied Expeditionary Force. This landing is a part of the concerted United Nations' plan for the liberation of Europe made in conjunction with our Russian Allies.

"I have this message for all of you. Although the initial assault may not have been made in your own country the hour of your liberation is approaching."

Landings, it is understood in London, were made in Normandy between 6 a.m. and 6.15 a.m., minesweepers clearing a way. Naval bombardments, in which U.S. ships took part, were carried out, and airborne landings made, first reports being described as good.

LANDINGS AT 6 a.m.

Allied bombers roaring over at dawn gave British people the first hint that big events were under way. Almost simultaneously the B.B.C.'s French transmissions began to warn French people to get away from coastal areas, to avoid roads, railways and bridges. "Do not gather in large groups," added the message.

Gen. de Gaulle, who has arrived in London and has had talks on military matters with Gen. Eisenhower and Mr. Churchill, is scheduled to give a radio talk to Metropolitan France.

D Day, 6 June 1944, as reported in the *South Wales Echo*. *South Wales Echo/Media Wales Ltd*

On 24 October 1944 the 'sea train' SS *Lakehurst* is seen once again, moored at the Import Wharf on the north side of Queen Alexandra Dock (later renamed the General Cargo Quay). On the starboard side of her navigation bridge is an anti-aircraft gun (commonly known as an 'ack-ack' or 'pom-pom' gun), while in front of the bridge is her forward gun. Behind the bridge is a set of twin kingposts with a mast in the centre on the kingpost bridge; behind again is a standard tri-mast derrick, used for the transferring of bulk stores. Two-thirds of the way along this vessel the gangway has been lowered, and to the left of this can be glimpsed one of the dock's shunting engines on No 2 Road. Between the engine and the gangway a motor vehicle belonging to Messrs Frazer & Co is delivering goods. The *Lakehurst* has a stern engine, and is riding fairly high in the water, so she has probably discharged her cargo and will shortly be at sea again. *Associated British Ports*

This next sequence of photographs was taken on 29 November 1944, and shows the loading of British 'Austerity' locomotives from the quayside of Queen Alexandra Dock, via floating cranes, to the receiving vessel at her mid-dock mooring. These Ministry of Supply 2-8-0 'WD' Class locomotives were designed by R. A. Riddles CBE and built by the North British Locomotive Co and the Vulcan Foundry. They are being shipped to France to help provide the British and American front lines with a steady supply of food, equipment, fuel, weapons, ammunition and medical supplies, and to evacuate the wounded to the safety of hospitals under Allied control.

Below The 50-ton MOWT improvised floating crane is about to lift one of the 'Austerity' locomotives using a 'lifting spreader beam', which enables the sling to be attached at each end of its load; this will distribute the weight of the engine and thus stabilise the load during the lift. Nearest the camera, at the quayside, is locomotive No 70812. *Associated British Ports*

Bottom The 'Austerity' locomotives are being marshalled into position by GWR pannier tank No 684 (on the extreme left).

Formerly Cardiff Railway engine No 32, and built as a saddle tank in 1920 by Hudswell Clarke to works number 1408, it was rebuilt by the GWR as a pannier tank with a parallel boiler in 1936, and withdrawn from service in 1954. On the right the 100-ton floating crane *Simson III* is in the process of lifting an 'Austerity' tender over to the 'sea train' *Texas*. On the left is the original Cold Store, opened in 1914 at the extreme western end of the north side of Queen Alexandra Dock; it had a quayside frontage of 300 feet, one receiving floor and three refrigerated floors each containing three chambers, giving a total storage capacity of 300,000 cubic feet. In 1938 this store was stripped of its refrigerating plant and was used as a general cargo warehouse; after the war it was renamed H Shed. *Associated British Ports*

Right Take a photograph from a high viewpoint and it becomes even more interesting, as demonstrated here. *Simson III* is about to lift an 'Austerity' locomotive from the Import Wharf. On No 1 Road is a selection of open trucks carrying wooden crates, and on the Stage Road is a line of more of these British-made locomotives. The cameraman has caught the attention of one of the group of men on the ground; by the look of them they are the engine drivers who have delivered the engines here, or they may be dockers. Next to the far crane is an armed 'Liberty' ship, while over in the centre, in Queen Alexandra Dock, the 'sea train' *Texas* is receiving a locomotive from the GWR improvised floating crane. *Associated British Ports*

Right The 'goose-necked' floating crane *Simson III* and its attendant tugboat are working together to manoeuvre the heavy load towards the waiting *Texas*. This 100-ton crane was designed to handle heavy and bulky lifts such as lock gates, boilers and large pieces of machinery; the hoisting, luffing and slewing actions of its jib were electrically operated from generators driven by steam engines, which also drove the propeller machinery. *Associated British Ports*

Top Spillers Grain Mill and its Grain Wharf in Roath Dock are seen here from the west, circa 1944. On the right the vessel at the Grain Jetty is discharging her cargo via the movable suction grain elevators. *Associated British Ports*

Middle After crossing the Swing Bridge over the Sea Lock of Queen Alexandra Dock, this road skirts the water's edge of the Entrance Channel. This 1944 view shows the Channel Dry Dock & Pontoon Company's entrance; beyond the flagpole, over to the left, is where the Channel Dry Dock's pontoon is moored, while on the extreme left can be seen the silhouette of the Pierhead Building, and the Entrance Lock gates of Bute East Dock. *Associated British Ports*

Bottom We are now in Bute East Dock, again circa 1944. In view is LCT (Landing Craft Tanks) No 999 with its coat of camouflage paint. In the background are the railway tracks leading to the coaling hoists on the west side of the dock. *Associated British Ports*

1945

Right Some time during the last year of the war we see Canadian tugboat 'CT-71' being lifted from the deck of a ship at berth in Queen Alexandra Dock with the assistance of the floating crane *Simson III*. In the background is a 'Liberty' ship bristling with guns. *Associated British Ports*

Below The floating cranes are being used again to load tanks aboard the SS *Empire Freetown*. This is an A34 Comet, used by British regiments in the final months of the war against Germany. The only British tank to make a significant impact on German armoured vehicles, fast and deadly and weighing 34 tons, the Comet was faster than the American Sherman tank and saw action at the Battle of the Bulge during the final push into Germany. They were equipped with a 600hp Rolls-Royce Meteor engine, a modified version of the unit that powered the Spitfire aircraft. They first came off the production line in 1944, and formed part of the 11th Armoured Division when 208 Comet tanks crossed into Germany, via the Rhine, on 29 March 1945. *Associated British Ports*

Dry hides from the SS *Empire Treasure* are ready for sorting in N Shed, Roath Dock, circa 1945. *Associated British Ports*

Bales containing valuable furs are being discharged by electric cranes from the SS *Empire Monfleur* at Roath Dock, again circa 1945. Further along, crane No 5 is discharging sawn wood from another vessel. *Associated British Ports*

Also at Roath Dock we see bales of sisal being transhipped from open railway wagons into the hold of the SS *Katholm*, destined for Denmark. Sisal is a fibre prepared from the leaves of the agave plant, and is used for making cordage and ropes, etc. On the right is an LMS open 13-ton wagon bearing the serial number 220918. *Associated British Ports*

Alongside N Shed, Stothert & Pitt cranes are unloading general cargo from the *Empire Mouflon*, again circa 1945. Between the legs of the movable cranes can be seen sheeted railway wagons; that nearest the camera has already been unsheeted ready to receive its cargo. In 1939 the Ministry of Shipping, in light of a forthcoming war, decided that all Merchant Navy ships built for the Government in British shipyards should have the prefix 'Empire' before the ship's name. Clearly seen on the rear upper deck are covered anti-aircraft guns. *Associated British Ports*

This general view was taken from the roof of the Cold Store, overlooking Communication Passage to the right, circa 1945. Beyond the ship on the right can be seen the timber storage buildings at Bells Wharf; behind these, standing above the other buildings, are the premises of the Bute Dry Dock Company. The vessels berthed alongside the cranes are at the Import Wharf on the north side of Queen Alexandra Dock. *Associated British Ports*

Above This battery of Lewis Hunter luffing cranes are in use at the Dowlais Iron Ore Wharf, Roath Dock, circa 1945. Between the legs of these hydraulically operated 3-ton-lift cranes are some steel-sided hopper railway wagons, used for the movement of iron ore to the nearby steelworks. *Associated British Ports*

Left Boxed oranges are being discharged from the open hatch of the cargo hold of the SS *Roxburgh Castle* to the waiting railway vans, under the watchful eyes of the 'tallymen' seen here on the left. Behind the oranges, part of the vessel's deck cargo is a ship's propeller. *Associated British Ports*

Left Another 'tallyman' (bottom left) is making notes; this time it is reels of paper being lowered into open railway wagons at the Import Wharf, Queen Alexandra Dock. These two men are having a laugh, but the driver of crane No 13 crane is watching carefully from the open window of his cab; it was his skill that turned the discharging into an easy or a hard job for the men below him. *Associated British Ports*

Unconditional Surrender At 3 o'Clock

HOSTILITIES END AT MIDNIGHT

Terms Presented By Air-Marshal Tedder

Channel Islands Freed

AIR CHIEF-MARSHAL SIR ARTHUR W. TEDDER

GERMANY SIGNED THE PEACE TERMS IN BERLIN AT 3 O'CLOCK THIS AFTERNOON.

This was announced by Mr. Churchill in a broadcast to the world shortly after 3 o'clock this afternoon.

The Premier added that hostilities would cease at a minute after midnight although the "Cease fire" had been sounded on all the fronts yesterday.

Following is the text of the Premier's announcement:

Yesterday morning at 2.41 a.m. at Gen. Eisenhower's Headquarters Gen. Jodl, the representative of the German High Command and of Grand Admiral Doenitz, the designated head of the German State, signed a pact of unconditional surrender of all German land, sea and air forces in Europe to the Allied Expeditionary Force and simultaneously to the Soviet High Command.

Gen. Beddell Smith, Chief of Staff of the United States Army, and Gen. Francois Sevez signed the document on behalf of the Supreme Commander of the Allied Expeditionary Forces, and Gen. Suslapatov signed on behalf of the Russian High Command.

THE SIGNATORIES

To-day this agreement will be ratified and confirmed at Berlin, where Air Chief Marshal Tedder, Deputy Supreme Commander of the Allied Expeditionary Force, and Gen. Tassigny will sign on behalf of Gen. Eisenhower.

Gen. Zhukov will sign on behalf of the Soviet High Command.

The German representatives will be Field-Marshal Keitel, Chief of the High Command and Commander-in-Chief of the German Army, Navy and Air Forces.

CHANNEL ISLANDS FREED

Hostilities will end officially at one minute after midnight to-night (Tuesday, 8th May), but in the interests of saving lives the cease fire began yesterday to be sounded all along the front and our dear Channel Islands are also to be freed to-day.

The Germans are still in places resisting the Russian troops, but should they continue to do so after midnight they will, of course, deprive themselves of the protection of the laws of war and will be attacked from all quarters by the Allied troops.

It is not surprising that on such long fronts as in the existing disorder of the enemy the commands of the German High Command should not in every case be obeyed immediately.

This does not, in our opinion with the best military advice at our disposal, constitute any reason for withholding from the nation the facts communicated to us by Gen. Eisenhower of the unconditional surrender already signed at Rheims, nor should it prevent us from celebrating to-day and to-morrow (Wednesday) as Victory in Europe Days.

Cardiff To Be Floodlit

Ban On Coastal Belt Remains

UNLESS there is a last-minute reprieve people living in the five-mile dim-out coastal belt of South Wales will not be able to see their buildings floodlit as hoped on VE Day.

Cardiff City is the only exemption.

The Lord Mayor of Cardiff (Alderman W. H. Parker) has been informed that the city may go ahead with its plans for floodlighting the civic and other buildings during the celebration days only. After that they must revert to the dim-out order.

People of Cardiff, like those in other parts of the country, stayed near their homes over the week-end and to-day ready to hoist flags and bunting immediately they heard the official announcement of VE Day.

Many, however, anticipated events. Most shop windows were gaily decorated with red, white and blue when they closed on Saturday night.

Above 'Victory Day in Europe', from the *South Wales Echo* of 8 May 1945. Cardiff will be floodlit for the celebrations, but not the towns along the coastal belt. *South Wales Echo/Media Wales Ltd*

Right In May 1945 the US floating crane *General Ike* is loading two 0-6-0 well tank locomotives onto the SS *Clan McMurray* at Queen Alexandra Dock. *Montevideo*, seen here suspended, was built by Hudswell Clarke in 1937 to works number 1683, and *Nellie*, built at the same works in 1938 to works number 1698, are en route to Egypt. *Associated British Ports*

Above These 20-ton private owner wagons, carrying the letters 'SC', belong to Stephenson Clarke & Associated Co Ltd; they were built by the Craven Wagon Co of Sheffield, and registered to the GWR. Also seen on the coaling roads in this June 1945 view is one GLM open wagon belonging to Gueret, Llewellyn & Marrett, en route to the moveable coaling hoists on the south side of Queen Alexandra Dock. The empty wagon in the bottom left-hand corner belongs to Binley Colliery, Coventry. *Associated British Ports*

Above right and right A mixed group of Naval officers and 'boffins' descend the quayside steps built into the retaining wall of the Queen Alexandra Dock Entrance Lock to the waiting motor launch. This was a 'Decca navigational test' in 1945, and was all very 'hush-hush'. Once they were aboard the cramped compartment of the Royal Navy launch, it sped out into the Entrance Channel. Whether the test was successful or not I do not know, but I bet there were a few queasy stomachs afterwards! *Associated British Ports*

Right and below right On 15 August 1945 Japan surrendered, and that day marked the end of a long and bloody conflict. 'VJ' celebrations were held throughout Britain, and the *South Wales Echo* carried the headline 'World Greets The End'.

These two photographs, taken during that month, capture the complete movement of a bale of wool from a Southern Railway 13-ton eight-plank open wagon, serial number 29171, to the nearby No 2 Shed, using a Ransome Rapier mobile crane. The wagons are on the Compound Road, and on the left is the rear end of No 1 Shed. The crane has a 360-degree slewing capability, is fitted with pneumatic tyres for travelling, and will have a lifting capacity of 8 or 9 tons. Beyond the wagon is another Southern Railway one, this time a five-plank wagon, serial number 34676. The wool will have arrived sheeted, as seen in the wagon on the left; these tarpaulin sheets may have been heavy and dirty, but they were waterproof. *Associated British Ports*

Left These bales of wool are safely stored away in No 1 Shed, Queen Alexandra Dock, in August 1945. The shed porters have plenty of work on their hands here, especially the man at the controls of the electric trolley, while the woman crane driver carefully and skilfully manipulates the controls of the mobile crane. This crane is fitted with solid tyres, has a fixed jib with no slewing capacity, and has a 3-ton lift capacity; however, its small size made it ideal for use inside warehouses. *Associated British Ports*

Top In the corner of Queen Alexandra Dock in August 1945 the SS *Empire Flame* is discharging bags of sugar into the waiting railway wagons. Chalked on the side door of the wagon on the left, an LMS 13-ton five-planked open, tare 6 tons 15 cwt, serial number 348945, is 'Empty 9-7-45'. Because of the awkwardness of the area, the dockers in the wagon in the centre foreground are using bag hooks to move the large, heavy sacks into place; these hooks could only be used when some damage to the bags was acceptable and the contents were not put at risk. The remainder of the wagons on the Water Road are various six-, four- and three-plank open wagons, sheeted and unsheeted. Once again, the driver of No 16 crane keeps a careful watch on his load secure in the bale sling. In front of the crane stands the 'tallyman', while behind him five dockers take a well-earned break. *Associated British Ports*

Middle The captured German vessel *Magdalene Vinnen*, on the left here in Roath Basin, is a prize worth having. *Associated British Ports*

Bottom On 17 June 1945 the surrendered German U-boat *U 1023*, now manned by the Royal Navy, sails up the Entrance Channel towards Bute West Dock, where it will be put on public display, moored alongside Robinson & David's warehouse (V Shed) next to the South Wales & Liverpool Steam Packet berth. These U-boats had a surface speed of 17 knots, but only 8 knots when submerged; they could stay submerged for 18 hours, cruising at 4 knots. They were armed with an 88mm or 105 mm deck gun, plus one or two anti-aircraft guns and approximately 14 torpedoes. Before 1941 they would appear in the middle of a convoy at night, but then radar forced the U-boat Captains to change tactics by staying submerged when going for the kill. *Associated British Ports*

Lest we forget

Above A respectful and sombre moment: berthed alongside H Shed, the former Cold Store, is the United States Army Transport vessel SS *Lawrence Victory*. Soon it will depart from Queen Alexandra Dock, taking back to their homeland the bodies of American servicemen who were killed in Great Britain during the war. *Associated British Ports*

Right A reminder to all of the sacrifice made by Cardiff Railway staff who joined the colours during the First World War, this Roll of Honour is in the entrance hall of the Pierhead Building, which was still occupied by the staff of Associated British Ports when this photograph was taken on 29 April 1987.

In the *South Wales Echo* of 27 January 2007, an article reported that, in the churchyard garden of St John's Church in the Hayes area of Cardiff, under the guidance of the Reverend Keith Kimber, it was hoped to erect a memorial to the people of Cardiff who made the ultimate sacrifice during the bombing raids on the City of Cardiff during the dark days of the Second World War. I wish him success. *Author*

CARDIFF RAILWAY:
ORDNANCE SURVEY REFERENCES

Cardiff Parade Station (Rhymney Railway)
ST188767 (no trace left)
Heath Junction (Rhymney Railway – original)
ST182798
Heath Junction (BR) ST182801
Heath Halt road bridge ST181803
Heath (Low Level) Halt ST181803
Ty Glas station ST171810
Occupation bridge (blocked underpass) ST173810
A469 Caerphilly road bridge ST166810
Phoenix brickworks ST168805
Birchgrove Halt ST166810
Occupation bridge (path to Porthamal) ST165809
Rhiwbina Halt ST159809
Whitchurch (Glam) station ST153809
A470 North Road bridge
(next to Whitchurch station) ST153809
Occupation bridge ST149809
Coryton Halt ST147809
A4054 road bridge (next to Coryton Halt) ST146809
Trackbed through Canal & Nature Reserve
ST144809-ST137813
Short length of trackbed between M4 and A470(T)
ST136817-ST135819
Tongwynlais station
ST134818 (no trace left – under A470(T))
Tongwynlais Tunnel (no trace left – under A470(T))
Cutting between Ty Rhiw and Glan-y-Llyn
(no trace left)
Portobello Quarry (near Ty Rhiw)
(no trace left – housing development)
Rhymney Railway (Walnut Tree Branch) underpass
ST127837
Taffs Well (BR junction) ST124833

Level crossing on NCB Nantgarw Colliery branch
ST124834
Moy Road bridge on NCB Nantgarw Colliery branch
ST123838
Glan-y-llyn station ST120841
Skew girder bridge over Cardiff Road ST120846
Nantgarw (Low Level) Halt ST118854
Bridge over A4054 (Cardiff Road) at Nantgarw
ST118855
Nantgarw Colliery (Industrial Trade Centre)
ST116859-ST120857
Nantgarw Coke Works (site of) ST117856-ST114859
ST116859-ST119855
Bridge at Rhyd-yr-Helyo Street ST116857
Gasometer on NCB Nantgarw Colliery sidings
ST114860
Nantgarw Colliery sidings ST109867-ST119857
Occupation bridge and NCB Colliery bridge ST110865
NCB Housecoal Sales site ST112864
Occupation bridge to Tyn-y-Wern ST109866
Occupation underpass to Ty Maen spring ST109867
Occupation bridge to Ty Maen ST109868
Heol Groes Wen Road bridge to canal towpath
ST107870
Upper Boat station ST104873 (now Industrial Park)
Rhydyfelin (Low Level) Halt
ST091880 (under A470(T))
Rhydyfelin Viaduct over River Taff
ST089881-ST088882 (demolished)
Rhydyfelin abutments ST088882-ST084885
Double arches with date above ST087882
Junction with TVR at Treforest
ST084885 (now school site)

ACKNOWLEDGEMENTS

I would like to thank the following for their help with these books:

Dr Don Anderson, Roath, Cardiff (former editor of *Ship Ahoy* magazine); Associated British Ports and staff, Cardiff; Brenda Brownjohn, *The Railway Magazine*, London; Lin D. Bryant, Pencoed, Mid Glamorgan; Sarah Canham, Research Centre Asst, National Railway Museum, York; R. S. Carpenter, Hollywood, Birmingham; Richard M. Casserley, Berkhamsted; Andrew Choong, Curator, National Maritime Museum, Greenwich, London; Stephen Cole, Local Studies Department, Cardiff Central Library; Chris Collard, Rumney, Cardiff (former editor of *Ship Ahoy* magazine); Katrina Coopey, Local Studies Department, Cardiff Central Library; Callum Couper, Port Manager, Associated British Ports, Cardiff; Michael Crabb, Easton, Portland; Viv Crabb, Pontypridd, Mid Glamorgan; John Curle, Wyke Regis, Dorset; Ian Daft, Easton, Portland; Ted Darke, Easton, Portland; John Davey, Managing Director, Stevedoring & Cargo Handling, Cardiff Docks; Martyn Farquhar, Portland, Dorset; Mrs Hillary Lloyd Fernandez (retired), Associated British Ports, Cardiff; Fleet Air Arm Museum, Yeovilton, Somerset; David Fletcher, Curator, Tank Museum, Bovington, Dorset; John Fry, Ely, Cardiff; J. and J Collection, c/o D. K. Jones, Mountain Ash, Mid Glamorgan; Brian Gambles, Birmingham Central Library; Glamorgan Records Office and staff, Cardiff, South Glamorgan; Stuart Hadaway, Asst Curator, Dept of Research & Information, RAF Museum; Michael Hale, Woodsetton, Dudley; *Harbour Lights* magazine, Swansea; Cliff W. Harris, Porth, Mid Glamorgan; Frank T. Hornby, Sutton, Surrey; Cliff C. James, Taffs Well, Mid Glamorgan; Mike Jarvis, Civil Engineers Dept, Associated British Ports, Cardiff; David Jenkins, Curator, National Waterfront Museum, Swansea; Derek K. Jones, Mountain Ash, Mid Glamorgan; Glyndwr G. Jones, Bromley, Kent; Mrs Jan Keohane, Archivist, Fleet Air Arm Museum, Yeovilton, Somerset; Harold Lloyd, Sully, Vale of Glamorgan; Doreen Luff, Cardiff; Tony Luff, The Grove, Portland, Dorset; Locomotive Club of Great Britain (Ken Nunn Collection); Keith Luxton, Taffs Well, Mid Glamorgan; David Mathews, Cardiff; Hywell Mathews, Pontypridd Library, Pontypridd, Mid Glamorgan; Media Wales Ltd, Editor and staff, Cardiff, South Glamorgan; Modern Records Centre, The Library, University of Warwick; Mrs L. Morris, Area Librarian, Pontypridd Library, Pontypridd, Mid Glamorgan; Steve Neal, Portland; National Railway Museum, York; Ordnance Survey Department, Southampton; Ordnance Survey Department, formerly at Pontypridd, Mid Glamorgan; John O'Brien, Pentwyn, Cardiff; Bill Osborn, Penarth, South Glamorgan; George Pearce, Grangetown, Cardiff; *Pontypridd & Llantrisant Observer*; Pontypridd Library staff, Pontypridd, Mid Glamorgan; Alun G. Powell, Rhydyfelin, Pontypridd, Mid Glamorgan; Royal Air Force Museum, London; *The Railway Magazine*, London; Doug Richards, Pencoed, Mid Glamorgan; Keith Robbins, GWS, Didcot, Oxfordshire; Ken Shapley, Associated British Ports, Cardiff; *Ship Ahoy* magazine, Cardiff, South Glamorgan; *South Wales Echo*, Cardiff, South Glamorgan; Graham Stacey, Secretary, LCGB, Egham, Surrey; Brian Stephenson, RAS Marketing, Ashford, Kent; Clive Thomas, Deputy Port Manager, Associated British Ports, Cardiff; Pat Thompson, County Hall, Cardiff Castle, Cardiff; Tony Woolaway, *South Wales Echo*, Cardiff; John Wynn (retired), Wynn's (Heavy Haulage) Ltd, Newport, Gwent; Peter Wynn, Wynn's (Heavy Haulage) Ltd, Eccleshall, Staffordshire.

INDEX